love her madly

love her madly

Jim Morrison, Mary, and Me

BILL COSGRAVE

DUNDURN
TORONTO

Publisher: Scott Fraser | Editor: Allison Hirst
Cover designer: Laura Boyle
Cover image: istockphoto.com/Pgiam

Library and Archives Canada Cataloguing in Publication

Title: Love her madly : Jim Morrison, Mary, and me / Bill Cosgrave.
Names: Cosgrave, Bill, 1947- author
Identifiers: Canadiana (print) 20190208384 | Canadiana (ebook) 20190209313 | ISBN 9781459746602 (softcover) | ISBN 9781459746619 (PDF) | ISBN 9781459746626 (EPUB)
Subjects: LCSH: Morrison, Jim, 1943-1971—Friends and associates. | LCSH: Singers—United States—Biography. | LCSH: Rock musicians—United States—Biography. | LCSH: Werbelow, Mary. | LCSH: Cosgrave, Bill, 1947-
Classification: LCC ML420 M62 C67 2020 | LCC ML420 M688 C67 2020 | DDC 782.42166092—dc23

We acknowledge the support of the Canada Council for the Arts and the Ontario Arts Council for our publishing program. We also acknowledge the financial support of the Government of Ontario, through the Ontario Book Publishing Tax Credit and Ontario Creates, and the Government of Canada.

Care has been taken to trace the ownership of copyright material used in this book. The author and the publisher welcome any information enabling them to rectify any references or credits in subsequent editions.

The publisher is not responsible for websites or their content unless they are owned by the publisher.

VISIT US AT

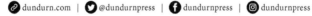 dundurn.com | @dundurnpress | dundurnpress | dundurnpress

Dundurn
1382 Queen Street East
Toronto, Ontario, Canada
M4L 1C9

To my wife, Julie

contents

prologue

Fall 1965

I'm leaving LA. We pledge to keep in touch — the first one to make some money will contact the other.

Jim's bemused. I've made arrangements to rendezvous with two strangers for a ride across the country. Another of my weird, seat-of-my-pants adventures that makes Jim shake his head and smile.

Mary hands me a ten-dollar bill as I climb out of her VW Beetle. I'm almost broke, as always. Jim's a little stoned, as always. And Mary — beautiful Mary — is practical and in charge. As always.

"I want this back one day, Billy Cosgrave," she says. "I mean it."

My ride arrives. My eyes are welling up. I hug my dear friends goodbye, tell them I love them, and hop into a car with strangers.

Typical.

Two years later, Jim would be on the cover of major magazines, rocketing to fame as an international rock star and sex symbol. Four years later, television, newspapers, and radio would stun the world with news of his shocking death in a Paris apartment.

During our last conversation after a Doors concert, Jim told me that Mary had gone to India. Mary — the girl Jim planned to marry, the girl I'd secretly loved — had disappeared.

Years later, I would find her in circumstances I could never have imagined.

My last visit to her home was as strange as the first. Mysterious Mary had disappeared again, along with her remarkable memories and her treasure box filled with Jim's personal notes, letters, and memorabilia. She was gone.

1: dream girl

Florida, 1963

Alligator Alley slices through the prehistoric Everglades, a straight cut from the Gulf Coast to the Atlantic. I have my thumb out in the torrid heat. Destination: Fort Lauderdale.

A battered pickup truck pulls over, with rusted, mud-caked shovels in the back. I climb into the filthy cab. The driver is wearing a dirty T-shirt and faded jeans. He's balding, with stringy black hair slick along the sides of his head. Crooked, yellow teeth, tobacco-stained fingers, nails chewed to the quick. He reeks of stale sweat and cigarettes. He looks at me with dull eyes. I ask him how far he's going. He mutters "Fort Lauderdale." It's going to be a long drive.

Hot air blasts through the windows. The baked dashboard is cracked, the windshield peppered with rock chips. The guy doesn't talk, he broods. The asphalt surface quivers in the visible heat.

A half hour later, there's a major furor on the road. *What the hell's going on?* Brooder slows down. Crimson-headed vultures are furiously devouring a crushed alligator that has met a semi-truck.

"Look at that!" Weirdly excited, Brooder brakes and pulls up beside the frenzied feast. Cutting the engine, he leans out his window. The vultures jerk their heads up from the festering corpse. A dozen cold, beady eyes stare at him, then plunge back into the carcass. It's dead quiet except for the sound of their beaks frantically tearing flesh, yanking out white strands of sinew. Horrible snapping sounds. Bits of blood and flesh spattered on their faces. Jesus, the stench.

"That's a nine-foot 'gator, probably four hundred pounds." He's talking to himself.

The guy watches too long.

The hot air is filled with the putrid odour of death. I start gagging. Brooder stares at me while slowly reaching for the ignition, a strange look in his eyes.

Who or what is this guy?

We drive on in an eerie silence through seemingly endless swampland. Finally, a hint of civilization appears: a faded ALLIGATOR WRESTLING sign, a rundown trailer park, an unpainted shack — CURLY'S BEER AND LIQUOR. A sideways Coca Cola sign hangs by a rusted chain. I begin to relax. Soon a suburb, then another, stretching out forever on this flattest of land. Buildings appear in the distance, their office lights twinkling in the dark blue of dusk.

Fort Lauderdale.

He drops me off at a gas station. With a strange, sardonic look in his eyes, he reaches out to shake my hand.

I get the key to the washroom and scrub my hands, thinking *I'll take the Greyhound back.*

I show the gas attendant the address. "Not too far," he says. "Straight down about four miles, then in three blocks."

I hesitate to stick out my thumb, but this time my ride is a pleasant-faced woman with bleach-blond hair looking just so. The scent of hairspray. Her companion in the back seat is a nervous chihuahua. "It's okay, Princess, it's okay," she tells the dog. Princess has the shakes.

The nice lady drops me off with a happy wave.

I walk the last three blocks to a tidy white house with green shutters and black street numbers. I have arrived at the house of Mary. Trembling with anticipation, I ring the doorbell.

———

Clearwater, Florida

Mary Werbelow. Dream girl.

I watch her from a distance. Her luminous beauty, the sparkling, intelligent eyes, porcelain skin, and sunny smile. She glows with optimism, self-confidence, independence. Her mesmerizing face, her Bardot pout, the liquid motion of her ballerina body, her swanlike neck. She is radiant. I am captivated by her, but she's older and doesn't know I exist.

Or ... *Did she just smile at me as she walked past me in the hall? Was she acknowledging me?* Not likely. She has the world cupped in her perfect palm. I'm imagining things.

A few days later I see her in the school parking lot, standing by her Volkswagen, talking to some girls and guys. She's engaged, yet somewhat aloof. She's ... *different.* She looks around and notices me watching her.

A week later, I hear an unfamiliar voice behind me. "Hello." And my world changes in ways impossible to imagine.

A brief exchange, then her smile. "See you later."

The next chat, a little longer. Later, a real conversation followed by "Would you like to go for coffee?"

Hell, yes, I would.

She picks me up in her Volkswagen, and an easy friendship begins. She treats me like a younger brother. She likes me, seems to trust me and see something different in me.

"But why did you leave home?" she wants to know. "What are you doing here?"

"I saved enough money to buy a ticket from Toronto to Clearwater to spend Christmas with some family friends. They have a daughter my age, and I met all her friends over the holidays."

Mary pays attention with her bewitching eyes.

"One of her friends said I could live in their guest cottage and go to Clearwater High with them. So I did, and here I am." (My mother wasn't thrilled but told me it was my decision. A divorced single mom with four kids, she couldn't afford to come and get me. And I knew it.)

"Don't you miss your family?" Mary looks puzzled.

"I do miss my family and friends," I say. "I mean, I love them very much. But I wasn't happy at my high school in Toronto where there had been zero tolerance for kids who were the least bit defiant," I tell her.

"And you were defiant?"

"Well, yes."

Mary laughs and claps her hands. "So, now you live in a screened-in porch?"

The guest cottage hadn't worked out. Luckily, I'd gone with a girl to a babysitting job and hit it off with the couple. The next time I met them I told them about my situation, and they offered to let me stay in their Florida room. In exchange, I did some babysitting and paid a bit for room and board. "They're great," I tell Mary.

She looks at me quizzically. "How old are you?"

"Sixteen."

I am smitten. She has no idea how dazzled I am by her.

She graduates and will attend St. Petersburg Junior College in the fall. At the end of school in June, I tell the school secretary that I'll be back in September to begin grade twelve.

Back in Toronto for the summer, I lie about my age to the Royal Bank and tell them I want a career in banking (I lie about that, too). They hire me as a teller trainee in a downtown branch right beside the legendary Sam the Record Man store. I love the colourful customers lining up at Sam's in search of the latest rock 'n' roll record ... so different from the lineup at my teller's cage. But the decent pay will give me enough to go back to Florida.

I think of the good vibes, the freedom. I miss my American friends, the easy lifestyle, the sandy beaches, the palm trees, the sparkling Gulf waters. Even going to school is fun. Why would I stay in Toronto for my senior year when I could graduate from high school in sunny Florida?

And I really miss Mary.

I need to be back in Clearwater by September fifth. I've saved most of my bank pay, and lucky me — a family friend who spent the summer in Toronto is driving back to Florida at the end of August.

Three days later we arrive in Clearwater. I get settled in my screened-in porch and head to Clearwater High to register for grade twelve.

"We were just looking at your file, wondering if you'd show up," the secretary says. "Welcome back!"

Mary has rented a tiny apartment while she attends St. Petersburg Junior College. Her parents have moved to Fort Lauderdale. I phone her.

"Come on over, Billy!" she says happily.

I borrow a friend's car.

Mary pours us tea and captivates me once again. *She's Audrey Hepburn*, I think to myself. Holly Golightly in *Breakfast at Tiffany's*. A little off-beat. Her mind sizzles. She is otherworldly, spiritual. What she doesn't know, she senses. She has a wisdom about her that says *I know*. She's older and wiser, but somehow there is a bond between us, and our unlikely friendship grows.

I love her mind. She speaks of meditation and soul and visions. She tells me things I never knew or imagined. She talks about her deep Catholic faith, about authors and theories and concepts. About art. There are books everywhere. She introduces me to new music. She glides about her apartment. Her laugh is captivating, musical, when something strikes her fancy. Her exquisite face lights up. She looks directly into my eyes as she speaks. I am enchanted.

She confides in me. And so I learn about her boyfriend, a guy named Jim Morrison — her soulmate. He's enrolled at Florida State University and hitchhikes to visit her on weekends. I never see her on weekends. Or meet Jim.

But then suddenly Mary is leaving Clearwater. She's moving across the state to join Jim. My cherished friend is leaving.

I am glum when we say goodbye. Will I ever see her again? We hug goodbye.

"Don't worry, baby, everything will be all right," she says.

———

I'm studying on my porch when her letter arrives.

Hi, Billy!

I'm staying at my parents' for a short while in Ft. Lauderdale. Why don't you come and visit? Here's the address. My parents have a guest bedroom.

xo
Mary

She tells me later that her mother whispered to her, "Mary, why is this fellow visiting you? He's so young."

We spend two glorious days driving around Fort Lauderdale. We hit the famous beaches and drive over and around the miles of canals. The wording on the city seal is "Venice of America." How that image lingered. Years later I would ponder the life-changing impact that the other and very different Venice of America had on the lives of Jim and Mary.

Mary tells me that she and Jim are more in love than ever. "Jim wants to get married," she says. He also wants to transfer to UCLA film school. He applies and is accepted for the second semester starting in January. "We'll get married in LA," he tells her. "You'll be the most beautiful bride in the world!"

Jim hitchhikes to UCLA to register and start classes. He expects to pick up Mary at LAX airport, but Mary surprises him. Independent and self-sufficient, she packs up her VW and drives 2,500 miles across the country to join him in LA.

2: jim and mary

"Billy, there is so much going on here. Jim is studying film. I have a job at UCLA. There are thousands and thousands of young people out here. The beach is amazing. There's so much music and art. And freedom. The weather is perfect. Why don't you come out? You will love it, I promise. You can stay with me as long as you want."

Mary's invitation is irresistible. I am back in Canada, attending Loyola College in Montreal and having major differences with the dean. We have reached an impasse. Mary's letter gives me an option in my life, and I leap at it.

Boarding a train in Toronto, travelling in economy class, I make the 2,300-mile train trip to Vancouver in three and a half days. I'll be hitchhiking the next 1,300 miles to LA.

The freedom of the road is beckoning, and the counterculture is hitchhiking everywhere. Abandoning their parents' values and rules, young women and men are hitting the road, alone or in pairs, with a backpack, sometimes a guitar, travelling for free, relying on the generosity of others. They share their songs and their dope. They trickle in to San Francisco and LA. Eventually, they flood in. A mixed bag of Beatniks, hippies, hipsters — peasant skirts and bell bottoms; turtlenecks and jeans; tie-dyed shirts and headbands. Protest songs and rock songs. Join the movement! Smoke pot, drop acid. Join the psychedelic revolution. People everywhere just got to be free. Rock 'n' roll bands, the voice of youth, scream into their microphones. *People power. We will change America. Fuck the establishment and materialism.*

Thousands of hitchhikers have their thumbs out … and so do I.

A car pulls over, a pleasant-looking husband-and-wife type inside. A brush cut and a beehive. Ozzie and Harriet. I hop into the back seat with my backpack. It's an easy drive from Vancouver to the U.S. border, the Peace Arch crossing. The light drizzle has become a heavy rain.

It's dusk at U.S. Customs and Immigration. "Your ID please," the customs agent says to the couple in the front. "Is this your son?"

"No, he's a hitchhiker."

He points to me. "Your ID, please." He looks at it, stares at me.

The officer is friendly to the couple and hands back their IDs.

He looks at me, not so friendly. "What is your purpose for travelling to the U.S.?"

"To visit a friend."

"What's your friend's name?"

"Mary. Mary Werbelow."

"And where does this Mary live?"

"Los Angeles."

"How long do you plan to stay with Mary?"

"She said I can stay as long as I want. So I don't know."

"Will you have any means of support while in the U.S.?"

"Not really."

"How much money are you carrying with you?"

"One hundred and fifteen dollars."

"Step out of the car, please." He has an unblinking stare. Tersely, he says, "Take your backpack and come with me." He tells the nice couple they're free to proceed.

Men with brush cuts stand behind a counter. Formal and polite. "Your ID, please, sir."

"What is the purpose of your visit, sir?"

"Step into this room please, sir."

Another brush cut is sitting behind his grey metal desk, stern, all business. "So, you're going to visit a friend, that's your only purpose. You don't know how long you'll be there."

"No, er ... no, sir."

"Do you know how you'll get back to Canada?"

"I'll probably hitchhike ... sir."

"How much money do you have?"

"One hundred and fifteen dollars."

Frowning. "And how much do you have in your bank account?"

"I don't have a bank account."

"Well, then, how much money will you have at your disposal while in the U.S.?"

"None, sir."

"Please remain seated."

He leaves the room. I have to pee. I stand up and turn the door handle. It's locked.

Five minutes later, stern man is back with an official-looking form. U.S. Department of Customs and Immigration: ENTRY DENIED.

"Come with me."

He opens the back door of an official car and ushers me in. He drives me back into Canada, stops, and opens my door. "If you attempt to enter the United States under false pretenses, you will go to jail."

I'm shocked and speechless. He leaves me on the side of the road in the pouring rain. Nice guy. Welcome to America! So much for the invitation on the Statue of Liberty: "Give me your tired, your poor."

Walking away from the Peace Arch border crossing, away from LA, away from Mary. It's getting dark as I amble slowly to nowhere. I don't have any family or friends in the West. What the hell? Now what?!

Two hours later, it's pitch black. My feet are killing me. I'm drenched, dejected, and desperate. I've got to get to LA. Got to get across the border.

The relentless West Coast drizzle continues. No lights on the highway. No distinction between black road and black night.

Then a pair of lights far off in the heavy mist. Getting bigger and closer. Headlights piercing the dense fog. Distant tires sizzling through puddles.

Focus. Make damn sure it's a pickup. Damn sure.

Bingo! I stick out my thumb.

The truck shrieks by, tires hissing like snakes, red tail lights disappearing down the glistening road. Suddenly, brake lights. The emerald forest lining the side of the road is illuminated by headlights. The truck is doing a U-turn.

The guy drives past, glances at me, does another U-turn. He leans over, cranks open the passenger window. Looks me over and sees a clean-shaven face, longish hair. "What the hell you doing out here in this shit? Hop in!"

I climb into the Dodge pickup with huge doors and a back seat. Soaked and shivering, I welcome the immediate comfort of the warm interior — like sinking into a hot tub.

The driver is in his midthirties, friendly. "My name's Bob." He's American. He has acreage and horses in Washington. He's bringing Canadian hay to his American horses. "It's better and cheaper," he tells me. "Where're you from?"

"Toronto. I'm heading for California."

"You've come a long way. What's taking you to sunny California?"

"A friend invited me to stay with her. She and her boyfriend moved to LA, and they love it. She wrote me to say I'd love it, too."

"You a hippie?" he asks. "What're you doing out here, miles from the border, looking like a drowned rat?"

I level with horse-owner Bob. "They denied me entry."

He starts chuckling. "So, you've travelled, what, twenty-five hundred miles, and now they won't let you into the U.S.?" More chuckles.

I swallow hard. "Bob, can I hide in the back of your truck to cross the border?"

He looks at me, then starts grinning. "Well, this is your lucky day, Canuck."

It turns out easy-going Bob loves a lark. "I cross here all the time," he says. "I know all the customs guys. I'm getting you through. Here's what we're gonna do...."

Bob pulls over, steps out into the drizzle, and removes the tarpaulin. He yanks several bales from the top row, reaches down to the row below, and wrenches two apart. "Squeeze in there, Canuck."

He piles the bales back on top of me. He grunts as he jerks the rope to tighten the tarp. I'm trapped and half smothered; the pungent smell of damp straw, rain clattering on the taut tarpaulin. I'm so tense I can barely breathe.

"Don't say a word; don't move a muscle — or it's over!" He thumps the side of the truck. "See you in the USA!"

I hear his cowboy boots crunch, the door slam shut, the engine rev. We plough through the rain. I'm shivering, wet, and blind. Sooner than I expected I can feel the truck slowing down, crawling to a stop.

"Hey, Bobby, enjoying the weather?" A hearty chuckle.

My heart is pounding frantically under the tarp.

"How're you doin', Jimmy? This goddamned rain never quits. At least my hay's dry."

"Go ahead, Bobby. See you next time." Gears clunk, the truck lurches forward.

Fifteen minutes later we're slowing to a stop. The rain has eased. Bob rips back the tarpaulin. "Welcome to America!" He's laughing away.

I'm still nervous, but I can't stop beaming. *California, here I come.*

———

Bob pulls into Blaine. "Celebration time — let's have a beer!"

"I'd love to, but I can't afford it."

"Well, hell, I can!"

This guy's good.

We take two seats on the worn oak barstools. A cute blond girl in a white cowboy hat plays pool with a bearded guy in western boots. Heartbreak country music is twanging away. Orange neon Budweiser sign. The bartender. Big hair, tons of makeup, ruby-red lipstick, and hoop earrings. A scent of cheap perfume. Thick false lashes; happy, sweet eyes. A couple of small stains on her crisp white blouse, her breasts straining the buttons.

"Hi, Bobby, how you doin', honey?"

"Not doin' anyone right now!" He guffaws.

"Not who … how? You need a new line, Bobby." She gives him a wink. "The usual, honey?"

"You got it, Sally, and one for the Canuck."

She smiles as she plunks down two pints of Bud in frosted glasses. Wrists ablaze with artificial jewellery, she reaches under the counter and retrieves a half-empty glass — lipstick on the rim, lots of fingerprints. Her personal glass. She takes the slow, measured sip of a professional drinker.

An hour later: "Last call, boys!"

Bob orders us one more for the road. Sally pours our drinks into two Styrofoam takeout cups.

———

Beginning to weave, Bob eases the truck into an all-night gas station/convenience store. He returns with a jar of pickled eggs and a dozen cold Bud. Slightly slurring, he says, "I'm gettin' too pissed to drive. Time for dinner."

I forget I haven't eaten.

Just ahead is a rest stop. He pulls in, parks, and pulls out a Marlboro. He lights a wooden match on his thumbnail. Draining the Styrofoam cup, he cracks open two Buds and hands me a few eggs. We start talking like strangers in a bar when they're drunk. Way too much beer, way too many pickled eggs. My head is spinning.

I stumble into the back seat. "G'night, Bob."

Bob stretches across the front bench seat. He's passed out in moments.

———

The morning sun pries my eyes open. *Christ is it bright.*

Bob stirs. "Morning, Canuck!"

We motor on for an hour past pristine pastures and farms. Here comes the rain again. We are both enduring terrible, head-splitting hangovers. Everything is excruciatingly loud — the rain pelting the windshield, the wipers thumping feverishly, the excited radio DJ.

"Well, here's the turnoff up to my ranch, pal." Bob pulls onto the shoulder under a stand of trees. "Too bad it's raining, but you'll stay dry under these. Well ... sort of."

"Thank you, Bob, for everything."

He shakes my hand and gives me a wink. "Good luck, Canuck. I hope you find Mary."

———

I'm standing beneath dripping trees. It's quiet out here. I listen to the rain splatting on the asphalt. I feel nauseated, dehydrated, shaky. *Thanks a lot, Budweiser.*

Christ, what was I thinking? I wasn't. I stick out my thumb.

An elegant black Oldsmobile purrs to a stop. "Where are you headed?"

"LA."

"Well, I can take you halfway there."

"Great. Thank you!"

What a comfortable car. Like a cozy hotel lounge with plush red velvet upholstery. It's raining harder now, and I'm glad to be warm and on my way, even with the worst beer hangover of my life.

The guy is speeding, eating up the miles. I'm dizzy and hungry. The heater is blasting hot air in my face. I try to stay focused on the road ahead. That is, until an excruciating pain erupts in my gut — a bulge advancing tortuously along my bowel. I'm twisting as the bulge continues toward its destination. There's instant relief as it thankfully escapes, but an unbearable sulfurous odour fills the car — a terrifying beer fart. I'm so embarrassed I can't look at the driver. Soon, I feel another building. I'm filled with horror. I clench my muscles in desperation, but to no avail. A second bomb, worse than the first, detonates. An overwhelming, eye-watering smell floods the car — the pickled eggs and beer combo. The desperate driver opens his window, gets soaked, closes it. There's nowhere to hide. He's a prisoner in his own car.

Mortified, I beg my guts for mercy. Teeth clamped, guts clenched, twisting in agony, I summon every muscle to tame the beast. But it's too late. This blast is lethal.

The car swerves onto the shoulder and jerks to a halt. There's a look of horror on the guy's face. "Sorry, dude, I can't take it anymore. You've got to get the hell out of my car."

I attempt a meek "I'm sorry." I try to speak but I can't because I'm trying so hard to suppress another equally unstoppable urge. *Please, God, please don't let me laugh* — an unanswered prayer. I see his bewildered expression as he watches my eyes bulging as I endeavour to mouth "Thank you." He peels away.

I picture myself receding in his rear-view mirror, enveloped in a sulfurous cloud. The image sets me off. I'm standing on the side of a road, laughing out loud, in the middle of nowhere, in the pouring rain. I'm embarrassed, hungry, and hungover — but I'm happy. I'm in the U.S., and I'm heading for the land of milk and honey.

And Mary.

There's a muted rumble, and a giant semi-truck barrels down the highway, its enormous tires sluiced with puddles, spraying sheets of water, the wipers furiously swiping at the rain. I stick out my thumb, and the monster slows, wheezes, and grinds to a halt fifty yards past me. The passenger door swings open.

"Hop on board, fella!"

I hoist myself up into a huge, warm, dry cabin. One of those fake scented green pine trees hangs from the rear-view mirror.

"Where you headed?" He's a middle-aged guy, his grey hair combed straight back, a weathered face and warm smile showing crooked teeth.

"Los Angeles."

"Well, I can take you as far as Portland.... You must be cold." He gestures to a box and says, "Help yourself to some hot coffee and sandwiches."

He's hauling railroad ties to a landscape company.

"You make money doing this?" I ask.

"It barely pays the bills." There's humour in his eyes. "I started out with nothing ... and I've still got most of it left."

So, there's me, laughing like hell, heading down the highway riding shotgun in a big rig.

When we reach Portland, I ask him to drop me at the bus station.

———

After four thousand miles of train, hitchhiking, and Greyhound, I have finally arrived in LA.

I step off the bus in late afternoon. The air is warm; the palm trees sway in the soft breeze. Next stop: Mary. I can't wait to see her. She has an unlisted phone number. My last letter simply said *I'm on the road and on my way.*

Drifting away from the depot, I come upon a sleazy-looking two-storey hotel with a large tinted picture window. Peering inside, I see a dark, busy lounge. I go in, sit on the last stool so I can observe the goings-on, and order a Bud.

Three animated girls occupy the stools at the other end of the bar. They're heavily made up. They're … *unusual.* Giggling, kibitzing, having fun. One of them puts a coin in the jukebox and comes back bopping to the beat. She winks at me. The place is bustling, getting louder. The flamboyant threesome orders another round. "And one for the guy at the end of the bar."

"Cheers — and thank you!"

"Slide on over and join us!"

Why not? They're happy and friendly.

They're also tipsy. "We're celebrating."

"Great, what are you celebrating?"

They point to the tall brunette. "It's Gerry's birthday."

"Well, happy birthday, Gerry!"

She gives me a big smile. "Thank you. What's your name?"

All three are in high spirits. "What brings you to LA, Billy?" they ask.

I tell them about Mary.

"Wait a minute … you've travelled four thousand miles to see this girl?"

"Uh-huh."

They love it. "She must be very special." After a pause, "Let's call her!" The girls are excited.

"It's an unlisted number. I only have her address."

They order us another round and ask for the cheque.

"Hey, why don't you come back to our place, spend the night in our guest room, and we'll drive you to Mary's tomorrow morning. We can have a few drinks. It'll be fun!"

We emerge from the bar just in time to see a spectacular sunset, the palm trees silhouetted against a soft pink sky.

As we arrive at their apartment, I realize what was unusual about them. These were my first cross-dressers. My initial fear evaporates when I see what fun, well-meaning people they are. They're simply helping a friendly stranger.

––––––––

The next morning, Gerry drives me to Mary's address in Hollywood. She gets out of the driver's seat and opens the trunk, handing me my backpack, then spontaneously says, "Give me a hug, honey. Here's our phone number. Once you're settled, give us a call. We'll get together and maybe come over and meet Mary!"

"Really nice to meet you, Gerry," I say. "Thank you!"

I wave as she drives off then head up the steps to find Mary's apartment. I ring the doorbell of the unit on my right. *Ding dong!*

My heart is racing, bubbling with anticipation. It's been so long since I've seen her.

There's no answer, so I try knocking. I have a sense that someone's standing at the other side of the door. "Mary? It's Billy."

The brass doorknob turns, and the door swings open.

Oh my God, it's not possible. She's even more beautiful. Chestnut-brown hair, long and loose; clear, luminous skin aglow as the sun over my shoulder catches her lean limbs.

"Billy!" She breaks into a radiant smile, clapping her hands. "You made it!" More laughs and hugs as she takes my hand, leading me into her cheery apartment. She sits down on the couch and pats the cushion beside her. "I can't believe you're here!"

She pops up to make us tea, and I follow her into the little kitchen. She puts on the kettle then leads me out the kitchen door to a tiny backyard. "Look at this, Billy, my very own avocado tree!" She is full of bliss. Her gorgeous face is animated. Her California tan is the icing on the cake. I love her with the innocence of youth, knowing that she is unattainable.

She's so full of enthusiasm. Telling me about the life she and Jim are living. Her eyes sparkling. "LA is fantastic, Billy. Jim and I love everything about it," she says. "There's so much happening here. We're so glad we came here!" She talks about the great vibes, the flood of young people, the creative wave in music and art, the excitement, the easy-going lifestyle, the flawless weather. "You're going to love it here, too, Billy. I guarantee it!"

I'm already pretty happy seated beside her on the couch, basking in her glow.

"When did you leave Montreal? How long did it take you? Where did you sleep?"

I begin the tale and am about to tell her about being smuggled across the border when the front door opens. And I finally meet Jim. He steps into the room, obviously surprised to see a guy sitting on the couch beside his girlfriend. He's maybe six feet tall, medium build, wearing jeans and a cream-coloured shirt. He has a heavy five o'clock shadow.

"Hey, baby, look who's finally here from Canada!" she says excitedly. "Billy Cosgrave, this is Jim Morrison."

"You made it." He reaches out, and we shake hands. He gives me a shy smile. "How're you doing, man? Welcome to LA."

I see kind blue-grey eyes. He has an easy-going, laid-back manner. "Finally, we meet. I've heard so much about you, Jim."

Another shy smile. "You, too, man. Let's have a beer, celebrate."

Mary's eyes flicker as Jim heads for the kitchen. She doesn't approve of alcohol.

He returns and hands me a cold bottle of Miller. "Welcome, man." He eases into the chair and props a foot on the edge of the coffee table.

"Billy was just telling me about being smuggled across the border."

Jim's eyes light up. "No kidding, man. You snuck into the U.S.?"

Conversation flows, meanders all over the place.

"Hey, man, can I get you another beer?" He talks in a slow, semi-Southern drawl. He seems interested in everything.

Mary asks about my battle with Loyola.

"I had ongoing conflicts with the by-the-book dean. Too many rules. I brought the letter that the dean wrote when I got suspended. I'll show you one day."

Jim grins. "Interesting. We have a rebel in our midst."

———

Mary is nodding off. We've been talking for ages. "I have to work in the morning," she says. She brings me a pillow and blankets for the couch. "This is your bed. Goodnight, guys."

"Hey, man, want another beer?"

"Why not."

We cover a lot of ground. I like him — a lot. He's charming, intelligent, and funny.

"Hey, it's almost two," he says. "I'm going to hit the hay, man. See you in the morning." He goes to the washroom then to Mary's bedroom, closes the door.

I curl up on the couch, so excited and pumped up it takes me forever to fall asleep.

The next morning, I wake up on the couch with my pillow and blankets. I listen to the birds outside the kitchen door.

Jim surfaces first — barefoot, jeans, no shirt. Sleepy lids, hair tousled. "Morning, Billy. You drink coffee?" He pours us each a cup then opens the kitchen door. He looks out at the avocado tree. "Look at that. They're ripe and ready to eat. Beautiful day, man. It's always beautiful in LA."

"Morning, guys!" Mary emerges in pyjama bottoms and Jim's T-shirt. No bra, no makeup. She takes my breath away. "Billy, I still can't believe you're actually here!" Laughing and clapping her hands, she gives me a hug. She is enchanting and whimsical.

She is also fiercely independent and practical. I learn that, much to Jim's dismay and disappointment, shortly after arriving in LA, ever-independent Mary moved out of his apartment and rented her own. Jim is shuttling between his place and hers. She quickly landed an office job at UCLA and takes art classes at LA City College; her conscientious and responsible side coexisting with her artistic and creative side.

She's sitting on the kitchen chair in the morning sun, brushing her long straight hair until it glistens. Then she heads to her bedroom, emerging in a white blouse and dark skirt. Brisk and purposeful, she grabs her small purse. "See you guys after work!"

Jim, who's rolling a joint, looks up, smiles, and waves.

I walk to the door and wave as she hops in her Beetle.

"What a girl," I say, coming back inside.

He exhales, grinning. "We're soulmates, man."

And I'm amazingly not even jealous of Jim. Mary is three years older than me, and three years in love with Jim. I'm amazed and grateful just to be entering their orbit.

———

On the weekend, Jim and Mary take me to Santa Monica Beach. No wonder youth are flocking here — the vast Pacific, breathtaking beaches, cascading waves. I see surfers and bikinis for the first time.

A few days later Jim borrows Mary's car to show me around. We drop her off at an administration building on the sprawling UCLA campus. Students wearing shorts stroll past palm trees and tropical plants. UCLA isn't Loyola, and LA sure isn't Montreal. I'm in heaven.

"What do you want to see and do, Billy?" Jim asks.

"Everything."

He grins. "Let's get going, man."

He takes me all over. To downtown LA, which is strangely fourteen miles away from the ocean, then along legendary Sunset Boulevard, past Hollywood and Beverly Hills and Pacific Palisades, to where it ends right at the Pacific Ocean. We turn right to Malibu, then head back along the Pacific Coast Highway past Palisades Park to the Santa Monica Pier. As Jim is parking the car, I notice how few people are on the beach now compared to the weekend.

"Let's walk down to Venice," he says.

"What's Venice?"

He points south from the pier. "A seaside town, down there a couple of miles."

Strolling along the shoreline, waves wash over our feet; the sun in a cloudless sky. Venice is very different, unlike the postcard image of LA. Ramshackle buildings, hippies, and bohemians hang around or wander about. The place is neglected. It has its share of weirdoes and derelicts.

"Why do they call this place Venice?"

"A developer had big dreams for this place," says Jim. "He built actual canals. You know, like Venice, Italy. I'll show you next time we come down here. Venice had mostly bohemians and immigrants living here, but there are lots of hippies now. It's sort of LA's Haight-Ashbury."

We drift until he stops to ask a guy for the time.

"Hey, we've got to get going to pick up Mary."

Back along the beach to Santa Monica Pier, Jim smokes another joint. "I love this place, man," he says. "Peaceful, laid-back, easy."

"Me, too," I say. "It's fantastic!"

I can see why Mary loves Jim. He's authentic and interesting. He's kind and loving toward her, polite and thoughtful. Extremely shy, he's unlike anyone I've met, with a remarkable mind crammed with knowledge and boundless curiosity. He will discuss anything. There's a certain Southern charm about him. He's courteous and well-mannered like Mary. Also, he's good-looking like Mary. They make a beautiful couple.

3: la times

I buy my very first copy of the famous *LA Times* and check the help wanted ads. There's one for telephone sales positions. I call and find out that the job involves cold calling and selling subscriptions to the newspaper. I picture myself working at this legendary newspaper as I head to the address for an interview. But instead of the stately building I envisioned, I arrive at a barren strip mall in a semi-industrial area. The stucco exterior is bleached and cracked. Crushed cigarette butts litter the pavement. I look at the mostly empty directory, white letters missing on the black felt, and find *C.J. Walters, 208.* I climb the linoleum-covered stairs and find a frosted-glass door halfway down the hall. When I knock, a thin girl with straggly hair opens it.

"Yes?"

"I'm looking for Mr. Walters."

"Is this about the sales position?" She has bored, indifferent brown eyes; a faded red dress hangs loosely on bony, pale shoulders. "Go into that room and sit down. I'll go get him."

A metal chair faces a cluttered desk on a scuffed, beige linoleum floor. A huge cut-glass ashtray is filled with butts. A cheap-looking brass nameplate sits on the desk: Mr. C.J. Walters. *What, the guy doesn't know who he is?*

In comes a man in a wrinkled white shirt with a yellowing collar, the sleeves rolled up revealing hairy forearms and a cheap Timex watch. He doesn't bother to shake my hand or introduce himself. He gives me the once over, then starts wheezing and hacking, his eyes bulging like a frog. Finally, he stops and clears his throat. "We do cold-call telephone sales. We sell three-month trial subscriptions to the *LA Times*. The more calls you make, the more money you make. I don't give a shit where you're from or what your experience is. Either you can sell or you can't." He hands me a sheet of paper to read. It's the sales pitch. "Memorize this." He tells me that the lure that reels them in is when you tell them you're a college student and "you only need to sell two more subscriptions to be able to pay for your education." A lit cigarette dangles from the corner of his mouth. In his shirt pocket is a pack of Camels — same brand my father smokes. I wonder how my dad's doing with his new wife and baby in Toronto.

"Come with me." Mr. Walters's left eye squints from the smoke. His finger flicks at a tobacco speck on his lip from the unfiltered cigarette. He leads me into a large windowless room with people sitting in cubicles giving the same pitch over their phones. The air smells of cigarettes and body odour. He leads me past incurious glances to an empty cubicle. "Here's a list of phone numbers. Start calling, see what you can do."

At the end of the day I've sold four subscriptions, and I didn't start until one.

"Hey, Billy, four on your first day. You can start tomorrow. I'll give you some pointers. There're always open cubicles, so you can work whenever you want. We pay your commission every Friday. Cash. No forms to fill out. Don't need your SSN, nothing. Just sell your ass off. You get fifty cents for each subscription."

Thank goodness things don't cost much ... like food.

But already I've got a job, and only a couple of weeks after arriving. My nest egg is down to thirty dollars. Now I can have some regular money to spend and contribute.

I head back to the apartment, where I share my job news with Mary and Jim. I describe my meeting and what I have to do.

Mary: "Congratulations, Billy. I'm proud of you."

Jim: "What a horrible job, man."

4: the academy awards

Another sun-drenched California day.

Jim and I are hitchhiking west on Pico Boulevard. A sky-blue Chevy Impala convertible picks us up. Top down, cruising in a warm breeze — driving in style to Santa Monica Beach.

The driver: "What do you guys do all day?"

Jim: "I'm finishing film school at UCLA. Otherwise, take it easy."

"Do you guys surf?"

"I love the ocean, but no, man, I haven't surfed."

"You should try it!"

"I like watching the ocean."

"What do you watch?"

"You know, the horizon, the colours, the rhythm of the waves."

The driver glances at him. "You just sit and stare?"

"Yeah, man. And I write."

"Don't tell me, you write movie scripts for Hollywood. You want to be famous, like all the other hopeless dreamers out here."

"No, man. You know, just my thoughts and poems."

I watch the driver's face in the rear-view mirror. His expression says "What a waste of time." He's snappily dressed. Fancy convertible, cocky attitude – I figure he's a salesman.

Jim gestures to me in the back seat. "He works for the *LA Times*."

Guy looks at me in the rear-view. "Doing what?"

"Sitting in a windowless hot room with strangers and their BO at a bank of telephones selling newspaper subscriptions."

"How's the pay for something like that?"

"I make good money, but it's a crummy job. The beauty is I can work whenever I want. Miss a day or three, then work twelve hours if I want."

The guy turns right on 7th, pulls over, and lets us out. "Good luck, guys."

"Thanks, man."

Jim lights up a joint as we wander past the Santa Monica Civic Auditorium, heading for the beach. A crew is hoisting a huge TV camera with an ABC logo onto a tower. Technicians swarm around. Hulking trucks unloading red carpets, cables, and equipment. A giant image of the gold Oscar is raised above the entrance. Spotlights are being mounted. Fences are going up.

"What a bunch of bullshit," says Jim.

He starts talking about New Wave French filmmakers, telling me about François Truffaut and other directors I've never heard of. How brilliant they are, discussing their techniques. Stuff I don't have a clue about. We're sitting on the beach now, watching the waves roll in, Jim explaining how the French are true filmmakers. "These Hollywood films are syrup for the masses. *Mary Poppins*. *My Fair Lady*."

"I thought *Zorba the Greek* was a pretty good film."

"You're right, man — a film with a great message. But it was a Britain/Greece co-production."

Jim has an amazing memory and encyclopedic knowledge, especially about films he's seen and studied at UCLA. He vividly describes details of a movie called *Breathless* by a director named Jean-Luc Godard.

"The guy's a genius. Go see *Contempt*. Man, the French are so far ahead of Hollywood. *Lola* — what a film!"

Jim wrote about everything he felt and observed. Constantly taking notes on the world. His ever-present notepad for his thoughts/poems. My first intellectual. From a stunning girl on the beach to musing about the universe; bringing up philosopher's names like Nietzsche, who, at that point in my life, I'd never heard of. Jim had read all of his books. Mary told me later that he could memorize pages and pages of writing and recite them back. Any time he showed me his writing, though, there was never even a hint of music. I had no idea that those poems would become world-famous hits. All that time spent together, and I never heard him hum a single note.

Jim rips out a blank page, writes down the names of films and directors, and hands me the list. "You have to see them, man. See what genius looks like — it'll broaden your horizons."

Me: "I'd like to go to the Academy Awards."

Jim: "What the hell for!"

Me: "To see all the stars and the glamour."

Jim: "Are you kidding me, man? They're phonies and squares. And their films are superficial sap. Besides, in a million years you'd never get in."

Me: "There's always a way."

I tell him about the time that I crashed a private party for Sammy Davis Jr. at the King Edward Hotel in Toronto after his concert at the O'Keefe Centre.

"Never heard of the O'Keefe Centre."

Of course he couldn't know that he and the Doors would one day play to a sold-out audience there.

Jim: "Sneaking into a private hotel function room is a hell of a lot different than crashing the Academy Awards." He laughs. "Impossible, man, impossible."

Me: "I'll bet I can. I'll bet you, uh, five bucks."

Jim: "I'm not going to take your money, Billy."

We have bonded. Both comfortable with silence. Gazing endlessly at the horizon. Thinking ... or not.

An hour later, walking along the beach, he lights a joint. "Hey, man, why don't you try some?"

Curiously, I still hadn't tried marijuana, in spite of my eagerness to try everything, to leap into the deep end.

"Come on, man, trust me, you'll love what it does to your head."

Why not? Mary does it. Jim smokes all the time. I trust him and feel comfortable with him. He's my friend. Who better to do it with?

"Just take a few tokes, Billy."

In no time I feel it — "Holy Christ!" Clarity. Like I've been looking through opaque glasses. I swear I can feel my mind expanding. Like a whale trapped under the ice, finding an opening and blasting through. I'm amazed and enthralled.

I look at Jim — I must look awestruck. A gentle smile spreads across his knowing face. *Welcome to my world.* Staring at the sea, his face reflects the amber of the setting sun. His eyes are more blue than grey in this light. He looks at me with an amused expression. "How do you think you'll ever crash the Academy Awards?" He is grinning at the thought.

We look at each other, and for no reason start laughing. My first contact high.

The *LA Times* buys us hot dogs and beer. We walk in the twilight to the pier and slide underneath. It's dark and strange. High tide. High us. Waves foaming as they wrap around the posts. Farther up it's even darker, but the sand is dry. We sit and listen to the motion. Mellow, drifting off. It's weird and isolating under here in the black. Soon, under this pier, Jim will write "The End" — a song about his heart-shattering breakup with his beloved Mary.

Jim: "We should sleep here sometime, man."

Little did I know….

We walk up the darkened sand to Ocean Boulevard where it meets Colorado. We stick out our thumbs, and two rides later we're back at Mary's apartment.

"Where've you guys been?"

"At the beach. Billy's going to the Academy Awards."

"What! How?"

I tell her my plan. "Oh, Billy, that's preposterous!" She laughs.

———

Mary has already left for work the next morning. Jim makes coffee, hands me a cup. "What are you doing today, man?"

"Gotta go find my Academy Awards suit."

"Seriously?"

"See you later, Jim."

On a down-on-its-luck side street in Hollywood, I find a combination pawn shop/used clothing store across from a couple of boarded-up storefronts. A bell tinkles as I open the door. Everything is layered in dust, except the bent old man crouched on a stool behind an ancient brass cash register. He glances up, then goes back to his crossword puzzle. Scratched, smeared display cases of tangled, worthless jewellery; in the back, stacks of yellow newspapers, magazines, and rows of books. A mixed scent of dust and mildew.

Under a water-stained arch is a smaller room with racks and racks of used clothing. The jackets and pants are impossibly jammed together. I find a black pinstriped suit, size 37, slightly wrinkled but hardly worn. The jacket and pants mostly fit. So far, so good. A ripped carton overflows with leather belts, like a pit full of snakes. The black leather size 30 belt works. Then, at a rack of stained, worn, and yellowed shirts, it's my lucky day. The one clean white dress shirt is crisp, the collar only slightly too large.

I head back to the hunched proprietor at the front of the store. The sun is attempting to shine through greasy handprints on the streaked front window. Has this guy ever cleaned anything?

"Excuse me. Do you happen to have any black dress shoes?"

He looks me up and down, at the suit and shirt in my hands. "You got a big date, sonny?" He chuckles and motions to me to follow him into a closet full of worn, cracked shoes. "What size?" I tell him and he starts rifling through his collection. He fishes out a pair of black dress shoes that mostly fit. "You need a tie, son." He shuffles off, comes back with a sorry-looking handful. I take the black tie. "Let's see what I can do for you." He adds up my purchases. "Tie, twenty cents; shoes, a dollar eighty; shirt, seventy-five cents; belt, twenty-five cents; suit, five bucks — that'll be eight dollars even," he says.

My eyes widen. "Mister, I don't have very much money, and this is really an important date," I tell him. "I work on commission and don't make very much. Could you round it off to five dollars?"

"Five bucks for all that!" The guy looks at me. "I'm already giving you a good deal. I need more than that."

"I'll make a deal with you," I say. "You give it to me for five, and I promise to come back in four days and give it all back to you, and you keep the five ... like you're renting it to me."

He looks into my eyes, musing. "Well," he says finally, "you sure as hell have the bluest eyes I've ever seen. Maybe they're honest, too. I'm going to trust you, even though I lost faith in most people a long time ago. I want to see those blue eyes back here in four days.... You got any black socks?"

He hobbles away and comes back with a pair, adds them to the used shopping bag. He stuffs the five dollars in his threadbare pocket. Raising his head up from his permanently bent back, the old man delivers a crooked grin with a twinkle in his eye. "Good luck, sonny."

———

Back at Mary's apartment, neither of them is home. I turn the shower on hot and hang the suit and shirt on the curtain rod, steaming out the wrinkles.

Finding a pair of scissors, I trim my hair back three inches. I buff the shoes until the leather is shiny, pull on the shirt, knot the tie, snug up the belt, slip on the jacket. I grab a beer from the fridge, take a swig and look in the mirror. A junior member of the Rat Pack is what I'm thinking.

The front door swings open. Jim comes in. "Man, what a sight. Where'd you get all that? You look good, man."

"It's my ticket to the Academy Awards."

Jim grins. "You're crazy, man. You might as well give me the five bucks right now."

———

The next day is the Oscars.

Mary is still at work. Jim comes in just as I'm leaving in my suit. Shaking his head, he says, "Well, good luck, man. I'll try to head out there later. See if you pull it off.... As if." Grinning, he says, "I'll be around the pier."

Dressed to the nines, looking like a million bucks, I'm hitchhiking to Santa Monica. A faded green '53 Pontiac pulls over. "What you doin' around here hitchhiking all dressed up?"

"I'm headed for Santa Monica."

"Is that where you work? Your car break down?"

I tell him my plan. He studies my face. "Are you serious, dude?" It's a knee-slapper. "You aren't putting me on, are you, dude? I'll be goddamned!" Laughing like hell, he gets such a kick out of it he offers to drive me all the way to the Santa Monica Civic Auditorium.

"Can you drop me a few blocks away?" I ask.

"Sure thing."

He pulls up to the curb, shakes my hand, and starts laughing again. "Good luck, dude!" He gives me a friendly whack on my shoulder. He's chortling as he drives off.

Catching my image in a store window, I can't help but grin: The Great Imposter.

Spotlights dance in the sky. Pumped up, hysterical fans are jammed together. Anticipation is crackling in the air. Cops and fences keep them away from the glass-fronted entrance. "Here comes someone! Who is it?" Excitement surging. A limousine crawls along the street to the entrance, emptying its precious cargo to screams and hollering from the adoring fans.

Even if I can squeeze through the seething mass to the front, there's no way I'm getting past the cops and security. It's getting darker. I edge away from the throngs and walk two blocks south, then double back and approach the building from the rear. The loading dock is jammed with trucks. Teamsters and workers bustle about. An impenetrable fence has been erected to prevent the hordes out front from getting to the back of the building, but curiously an opening at the rear leads to the loading dock. A threatening NO TRESPASSING / VIOLATORS WILL BE PROSECUTED sign is posted. It's dark now as I move casually toward the trucks, not even eliciting a glance from the preoccupied truckers and their helpers. I edge up beside a truck parked snugly near a set of stairs that lead to a back door. *Damn.* A security guard who hasn't seen me in the shadow of the truck is guarding the door.

Roars suddenly erupt from the front of the building. Another star is arriving on the red carpet. I hear a major commotion from behind: scuffling shoes on concrete. Running. Shouting. *Shit — I'm caught! It's the cops.*

But it's a stampede of photographers chasing a limousine pulling into the back entrance. It eases to a stop between the truck and the stairs. I'm squeezed beside the back passenger door and the stairs — trapped. An army of press swarm the door as it swings open: "Hey, Jimmy, Jimmy, give us a wave. Hey, Jimmy, give us a smile!" Jimmy gets out of the back seat. It's pandemonium. He's hustled up the stairs with an eruption of shutter clicks and flashes. I'm jammed right behind him, getting shoved up the stairs by the surging photographers. Jimmy swivels, doffs his hat, gives them what they want — his famous grin. His face is beaming, brown eyes gleaming, and I'm thinking, *Way shorter in real life.* I'm still right behind him as the door suddenly flings open.

It's bedlam. Press yelling, pushing and shoving, blinding flashbulbs. And I'm swept through the back door with Jimmy Durante and his handlers as the door slams shut on the frenzied photographers.

Christ, I'm in! Now what?

I'm a few feet from the famous bulbous-nosed celebrity. "Right this way, Mr. Durante," and they disappear behind some props.

Heavy, deep red curtains; I'm backstage. What a buzz. Busy, frantic people move about. Nobody gives the young guy in the suit a second look. There are the sounds of an orchestra tuning up, mics being checked. People are scurrying about, tense and purposeful.

Moving to the side of the stage, I edge the thick velvet curtain open to reveal a sea of seats, the room surprisingly dimly lit, with just a few people sitting in them. My heart is racing. *I'm in the bloody Academy Awards theatre!* Everybody is too busy to notice me. I walk down the stage stairs and purposefully up the aisle toward a growing hum. The odd person is checking row numbers, looking for their seat; but where is everybody? And where the hell am I going to sit?

I scan the seats. I've got to figure this out. The hum is getting louder as I get to the last row and the doors leading into the lobby. I almost collide with a couple of tuxedoed guys as they open the door to a cacophony of voices. When there are that many people talking at once, no words are distinguishable, but their faces sure as hell are. There's Rex Harrison talking to a dazzling woman sipping

champagne. What! It's her. Audrey Hepburn! A thin-necked porcelain doll, she looks so … *fragile*.

*Quit looking at her, you idiot, get a drink. You're the only one not
holding a drink.*

I make my way to the closest bar, squeezing past faces I recognize, and get in the short lineup. The place is jammed, people hugging and kissing and telling each other how beautiful they look.

The atmosphere is electric, crackling with excitement and anticipation. I look back at Audrey greeting a stunning, voluptuous
woman — Sophia Loren. She's almost twice the size of Audrey, but
the same height.

Quit staring, for Christ sake! Squeeze past that guy. "Excuse me,"
I say to Anthony Quinn. Get to the bar.

The female bartender asks, "May I help you, sir?" Man, even
the bartenders are gorgeous. Do they have makeup artists, too?

"Yes, please. A glass of champagne."

She pours it and hands it to me. "Your ticket, please," she says
with a warm smile, a speck of red lipstick on her blinding white teeth.

What! You're supposed to have a drink ticket? Shit!

I freeze. Returning her smile, I reach slowly inside my jacket,
pretending to look for my ticket. Then I reach into the other inside
pocket. Panic. My heart is pounding. The gig's up.

"Here, he can have one of mine." A slender arm wearing a
shimmering diamond bracelet slides past me and hands the bartender a ticket.

I turn around wearing a smile, champagne flute in my hand. I
say thank you very much to the most enchanting, smoky-blue eyes

I've ever seen. They belong to Lee Remick. She is stunning, mesmerizing. I saw her in *Days of Wine and Roses*. She is much more beautiful in person.

"You're welcome." She smiles. I tip my glass, sip my champagne, grin at her, and edge away from the bar. She gives me another smile, eyebrow slightly raised. To this day I believe that she knew what I was up to and jumped in to save my cover.

I'm giddy. *I did it. I'm at the Academy Awards.* I can't wait to see the expression on Jim's face.

More people are cramming into the reception, the crowd outside roaring every time a limo pulls up. Everywhere I look — behind me, beside me, in front of me — there are famous faces. Everyone is jammed together. Celebrity central: Steve McQueen, Angie Dickinson, Judy Garland, Bob Hope, Julie Andrews, Joan Crawford (I'll be sitting beside her and kissing her cheek in a few months). Look, it's Richard Burton: worst complexion ever. As short as Jimmy. In fact, they all look smaller in person. (I will meet Dick and Liz in Puerto Vallarta eight years later.)

The place is buzzing and pulsating. You can feel the energy. The perfumed women in their diamonds and shimmering dresses, perfectly coiffed, not a hair out of place; the tanned men in their tailored tuxedos. These handsome, beautiful people are radiating charm and grace in their rarefied circle. The faces of the aristocracy glimmer and glow.

I've drained my glass, and I notice that people are leaving barely-touched drinks on high-top tables: can't give your acceptance speech drunk. I glance around, put my empty glass down, and take the almost full flute beside it. Nobody notices.

I do it again — and again. I'm feeling light and relaxed, floating here in the middle of this sea of celebrities. Hell, if I nod and smile at them, they even smile back. *Here's to us winners.*

"Excuse me, sir." A hand lands on my shoulder. It's a man in a tux — the only guy in the place not smiling. "How are you to-night, sir?"

"Terrific, thank you." I've got a buzz on. Smooth and easy. This is going perfectly. As soon as I find my seat everything will be jake. Let the ceremonies begin!

"May I see your invitation, sir?"

"My invitation?"

"Yes, your invitation." Still not smiling.

I can hardly breathe. Reaching into my jacket pocket, I fumble about. I make a big deal of searching my pants pockets. Then I give him my best easy-going grin.

"Come with me, please."

"Is there a problem?" Champagne-fuelled bravado.

"Take a look around at what all the men are wearing."

A flare ignites in my stomach. I look around at the sea of tailored tuxedos as far as the eye can see. Then me in my thrift-store black pinstripe suit.

"You can't find your invitation because you don't have one."

I've been "discovered" at the Academy Awards, in the midst of Hollywood aristocracy. But not like in the movies.

"Come with me, sir."

I'm given the boot. Tux escorts me to the glass entrance doors, past the cops and security men, and into the mob of fans. "Look! Who's that?" A gaggle of excited girls are looking at me. "Who is it? Can we have your autograph?"

"Um, sure," I say. I scribble my name on their fan magazine and melt into the crowd, feeling both deflated and ecstatic. *Man, I DID IT! What a rush!*

But suddenly I'm on the outside looking in. Stunned, I stroll three blocks to the beach in my shiny black shoes, suit to match. Night lights are twinkling on the water. I scan the dark sand, look down the beach. Maybe he's down there at the pier. What the hell, nowhere else to go except the apartment. Still pumped, I head down the boardwalk. Weird glances come from the night creatures: staggering drunks yelling at nobody, helpless druggies with vacant stares, a couple of long-haired blond guys with surfboards and dripping wetsuits emerging from the surf. I'm thinking, *Wow, what a trip, surfing in the dark. I want to do that.* They see a young guy in a black suit, tie loosened, ambling toward the pier.

Getting close, I smell the aroma of fried onions coming from a hot dog stand. Suddenly, I'm hungry. Surprised the guy's still open. I order a hot dog. The guy in the greasy apron gives me a curious look. "Wanna Coke to go with it?"

"No thanks." Half an hour ago I was sipping Dom Pérignon champagne.

I see Jim sitting on the sand near the pier, staring out to sea. "Jim!" He doesn't hear me. Either because of the sound of waves breaking and washing under the pier, or he's lost in thought.

I'm right up beside him now, standing there in my suit.

"Hey, man," he says.

I'm grinning, excited as hell. "You owe me five bucks."

"No kidding, man!" His face glows as he fires up a joint.

I tell him the story. He's looking at me, an amused expression on his face. When I tell him about the excited girls asking for my autograph his eyes widen and he breaks out laughing.

Two years later Jim would emerge from a sold-out Doors concert at the same Santa Monica Civic Auditorium and be swarmed by a mob of girls asking for his autograph.

———

A couple of days later I'm back at the old man's shop. The small bell attached to the door tinkles, announcing my arrival. Waiting by the antique counter, I hear shuffling. I hand the bent old man the shopping bag with my Academy Awards costume. His mouth is caved in, but he delivers a toothless grin. His false teeth are missing. Incredibly, he has one tooth, on the bottom right. What a sight. Mustn't be expecting any customers today, or he's past caring.

"I figured I'd see those blue eyes again," he says, not bothering to check the bag.

"How was your date?"

"Unbelievable."

5: takin' it easy

Mary is an artist. She paints, she dances. She is curious about everything. Observant and analytical, she seeks answers and the truth. She and Jim are peas in a pod. Her apartment is tidy, clean and bright, and I'm a careful guest. Everything has its place. She has books everywhere. When she reads, she is totally focused. I love the look of concentration on her face. Jim is also addicted to reading: "Hey, listen to this." "Did you know that … ?"

They're both so damn smart; discussing psychology, human behaviour, movies, art, philosophy. I feel woefully uninformed. All these names they bring up that I barely recognize or have never heard of … but wish I had. Jim is always courteous and respectful.

He is so well-read and knows so much, yet he talks to me as an equal, answering my questions, asking, "What do you think?" And he cares what you think. His invariable response — "interesting." He's a gentle guy, and for all his intelligence and confidence, he is so very shy.

Having a meal with Mary, I comment on Jim's remarkable intelligence.

"He's read tons of books," she says. "He has a genius IQ — 148. And guess what?" She pauses and grins. "Mine's higher than his."

One night, the three of us are at the kitchen table. Jim rolls a joint, lights it, and passes it to Mary. She has a toke, passes it to me. The three of us are soon pleasantly stoned. I remind Mary how in one of her letters she wrote that she was determined to stick to her Catholic guns and not have sex until they were married. They laugh at their innocence. That they were both virgins when they met. He teases her lightly about her religious faith and guilt. Mary talking about God and spirituality. A devoted Catholic.

"Tell Billy about that time you agreed to come to church with me. How do you explain that? If it wasn't a spiritual experience, what was it?"

Jim nods his head. "That was strange, man. The light hovering in mid-air."

Slowly, the story unfolds.

Mary had been trying to convince Jim. Imploring him to believe, telling him about the love of God, about the Catholic religion. "I don't buy it" was Jim's fundamental attitude.

Jim was searching for truth and meaning elsewhere — in books, in his mind. And then, late one night, while they were in Florida, Mary coaxed Jim. "Please, Jim, just come to church with me right now. There will be no one there. Just you and me. The door is always open."

Jim reluctantly agreed.

They drove to her church, and not a soul was in sight. Heavy wooden doors groaned open as he followed her in. Suffering faces of stained glass saints softly illuminated by the muted street light. Their footsteps echoed off the ancient wood floor, bouncing around the cavernous church. Mary led Jim to a pew halfway up. She slid in, motioned for him to sit down. A trace of incense was in the air. It was quiet as a tomb. Jim was gazing around.

"Why are so many candles lit over there?" Jim pointed.

"Shhh! — you have to be quiet, Jim!"

"Why, there's no one here?"

"Shhhh. You have to be respectful. People come and light a candle, make an offering, and say a prayer."

"How come there are so many?"

"Lots of people believe, Jim … and pray."

Mary reached down and rotated the padded prayer board. Got down on her knees and prayed. Palms together, eyes closed, she beseeched God to let Jim believe.

"Please, God, please help me. Show Jim you exist."

Jim was bored, looking around. *What a lark. All these statues. People worshipping marble. Believing what they're told.* There was a portrait of Jesus, fair-skinned, blue-eyed. He thought he was a

swarthy-skinned Jew. *Man, is this place quiet … and dark.* There
was a dim red light over the exit door. Mary was still praying.

Jim shifted. Looked up. A pinpoint of light. He looked away,
looked up again. The ceiling must have been three storeys high.
The pinpoint became a little brighter. *Was that there before? Must've
been,* he thought.

He looked up again. *What the hell's happening?* He looked
at Mary, head bowed, eyes squeezed shut. The dot got brighter,
slightly larger. *Who's fucking with the lights, man?* He looked up
again. *Where the hell's the extension cord for the light up there?*
His eyes scanned left and right. There was no cord. Nothing attached to the light. But it wasn't even a light bulb. It was round
and glowing. Suspended in mid-air — growing brighter, more
intense. Jim looked up in awe. He took a quick glance at Mary.
The thing was so fucking bright he couldn't look directly at it.
Mary was now staring up in wide-eyed wonder at the blinding
light, transfixed.

Jim was stupefied. *What the fuck?* He leapt up and headed for
the door. Mary followed.

Jim stood on the concrete stairs, heart racing. "What was that?
Did you see that! What the hell's going on?" Breathing slower.
Calming down. Looking back at the closed door, he moved toward
it and cautiously opened it. They looked inside. Dead still. No mo-
tion, no light, not a sound or a soul in sight. Bathed in darkness.
Flickering candles along the side wall. Up there? Nothing.

The story ends and we move from the kitchen into the tiny living room. Jim and I lounging on her thrift-shop sofa. Across from

us, Mary, legs tucked under her in the chair, looks at us. "It was a sign from God," she says calmly.

I look at Jim. "What do you think it was?"

"I, ah, don't know, man." He lights up another joint and hands it to me. "But it was real."

———

We're at ease and comfortable with one another — Mary working at UCLA; Jim studying at UCLA; me heading off to my high-profile job selling the *LA Times*. Meals in the apartment or at cheap restaurants. Hanging out; reading; discussing events, ideas, life. Weekends at the beach. Life is easy and breezy.

But there are dark clouds on the horizon.

Mary has signed with an agent who lands her a job dancing at a hot nightclub on Sunset Strip. Jim thinks it's demeaning, and he's pissed off. He wants her to finish college. But Mary wants to be a dancer, and she is nothing if not determined.

In no time she becomes the star go-go dancer at Gazzarri's Hollywood A Go-Go. Jim thinks it's cheesy. She is eventually crowned Miss Gazzarri.

Something's up. I can sense it.

After a couple of days, I ask, "Mary, where's Jim?"

She fills me in.

The two of them were about to enter the apartment, when she stuns Jim. "Jim, you're not coming in. You have no money, no idea what to do. It's been long enough. All you know is books.

Go and discover yourself. I have to find myself, too, then we'll get married."

I'm shocked, surprised, and confused. A sadness washes over me.

His parents had cut him off when school ended, so he could no longer pay rent and had given up his apartment.

"Where did he go?" I ask.

She has a far-off look in her eyes. "He said he was moving to the beach."

The next day I hitchhike to Santa Monica Beach and find Jim sitting on the sand, writing on a notepad, smoking a joint.

"Hey, man, nice to see you." His eyes are pained. "Look at those waves." He seems utterly alone and vulnerable. Rejected by his soulmate, the woman he has adored for three years, he is despondent. His sadness is palpable.

6: sunset strip

Hitchhiking to Sunset Strip. An endless parade of peasant skirts and bell bottoms — long-haired, hope-filled hippies. Pulsating crowds promenading down Sunset Boulevard. Traffic crawls by — horns amiably honking, anonymous arms extending out the window to share a joint. It is a time when spontaneity is the norm. There is an openness, an excitement. Change is possible. "It's all good, man."

Good vibes, until …

A shiny black car nudges into sight. Someone yells "That's Richard Nixon! Fuck you, you asshole!" My polite Canadian-self cringes. I look at the guy in the passenger seat, and Christ, it really is Nixon! Instantly, the crowd's antennae are crackling. They scream expletives at him. "It's shithead Nixon!" someone yells, a group surging toward his car. His face dons a wooden mask; a tight-lipped phony smile. A solitary man surrounded by a sea of hate. The car abruptly turns right and slithers away. Classified recordings would reveal that Nixon engineered the collapse of secret peace talks organized by President Johnson because peace threatened Nixon's presidential bid. Nixon won, the war was prolonged, thousands of Americans and Vietnamese were killed and maimed. Nixon was guilty of mass murder but was never charged.

Sunset Strip: a river of hopeful, stoned youth, guilelessly sharing their vision. *Peace and love, brother. We can do it, man.*

Weaving through the ubiquitous scent of weed, squeezing my way through the overflow lineup at the hottest rock 'n' roll club in Hollywood, the Whisky a Go Go, where incredibly only one year later Jim would be onstage singing "The End" with the as yet non-existent Doors. And where Bruce Palmer, a solitary kid who used to practise his guitar in our basement, would play on the same stage, on the same night as Jim, with his bandmate Neil Young: the Doors and Buffalo Springfield live at the Whisky.

I walk into Gazzarri's Hollywood A Go-Go nightclub with its flashing lights. On the dance floor, spaced-out frantic dancers with flailing arms; bathed in spotlights, the go-go girls in their miniskirts. The Hollywood club is chaotic and loud. A hotspot on Sunset Strip, a block from the Whisky. Live and loud music. Beautiful go-go girls — the Gazzarri Dancers. One of them is impossibly gorgeous. Her ballet-toned body glistens in the nightclub heat. Consumed by her joy of dancing, her eyes electric, flashing. She is spellbinding. Rhythmic, sensuous. Staring out into space, oblivious to the riveted male eyes. Mary in her white go-go outfit, the fringes accentuating her sensuous moves. Her perfect body. Her radiant smile. Her silky, liquid chestnut-brown hair. Her dancing intense, ecstatic, feverish. *This is for me, patrons — not for you.* Sort of.

Mary. Innocent, alluring, unapproachable, unattainable. She drives men crazy, including the bespectacled guy grinning at me from his table.

"Excuse me, sir. My employer would like to buy you a drink." A middle-aged man is standing at my table in an impeccable suit, jacket dutifully buttoned. He gestures at the thin, nerdy guy sitting at their table nodding at me.

Suit Man says, "I'm George. May we join you?"

Since Mary got the job at Gazzarri's, she has introduced me to the employees as her Canadian cousin. Most evenings I end up here at the club. The staff gives me a good table where Mary joins me between dance sets. She's endlessly hit on. "No thanks … I'm with my cousin Billy." If she accepts an invitation to some after-hours Hollywood party, the proviso is simple: "Billy comes with me."

George goes back and brings his "employer" over to my table. A guy, twentysomething. He introduces him as Hunt. I shake his hand. He grins eagerly. Drinks are ordered. Mary finishes another frantic set, comes over — out of breath, sweat on her forehead, hair damp — like she's just had sex. Hunt looks like he's going to faint. I introduce them. They shake her warm hand. She gives them her radiant smile, her lilting laugh. Add two more to the smitten list. No wonder Jim got so angry when she quit her office job to become a dancer at a hotspot nightclub. His girlfriend, the girl he plans to marry, on display to guys ogling her every night. You can hear them panting.

George picks up the tab; I thank him and head for the exit. The two follow me out. "Would you like a ride home?" asks George. He leads me to an enormous shiny red Rolls-Royce, parked illegally. George becomes the chauffeur, opens the back door. I get into the back seat with Hunt. What's going on here? Hunt really is George's boss?

"Are you hungry?"

I always am. We head to a late-night diner.

The Rolls glides along Sunset, the good-natured crowds spilling onto the street. Suddenly, Hunt pushes a button in the ceiling and a police siren wails from the roof of the Rolls. Hunt inappropriately cackles as pedestrians freeze and stare.

What the hell? Get me out of here!

Then he does it again and again … and again.

People stare as the Rolls-Royce pulls into the diner parking lot. I make up for lost meals. George picks up the tab. They drive me home. George asks if they can meet me the next night at the club. They show up. Mary takes a break, comes over. Hunt is almost drooling. Hypnotized.

When Hunt goes to the men's room, George explains that Hunt is obsessed with, in love with, Mary. This is why he approached me. They had seen Mary frequent my table. He then asks, "Would you consider being friends with Hunt?"

Huh?

A couple of nights later the twosome shows up again. Same routine — join my table, meet Mary, hop in the Rolls, idiotic siren, a late meal, drop me off.

The next day I hitchhike out to Venice and find Jim. He's broke, but I've got my pay from the *LA Times* — enough to provide us with a hamburger and a beer each and cigarettes. Jim tells me he found a roof to sleep on.

The time we spend along Venice Beach blends seamlessly from one day to the next. Drifting along in easy conversation. Just hanging out. There's a strange blend of people out here — reprobates, misfits, some hippies, some bohemians — peaceful, mostly pleasant people getting by … barely.

Jim may be broke, but he seems to have an inexhaustible source of weed. He is also dropping acid. With his film school degree behind him and the endless summer before him, he doesn't seem to be concerned about anything. He doesn't talk about getting a job. He's on summer holidays, sitting on the sand, staring at the sea. All he wants to do is what he's doing: write, dope, acid.

Despite being extremely shy, he is charming and funny. Our conversations are wide-ranging. He bristles at the abuse of power. Distrusts authority and despises the power it bestows. He tells me about his father, a high-ranking navy admiral who loves the military. A firm believer in discipline, he subjected Jim to rigid punishment when he "misbehaved." He gave Jim his middle name,

Douglas, as in Douglas MacArthur, the legendary five-star general.
When he is later interviewed, Jim says that his father is dead.

———

At Gazzarri's a few days later, they are there again — the odd duo.
The gentleman chauffeur and the peculiar young man. Same routine, except this time George tells me he is authorized by Hunt's
father to offer me a job. "To be Hunt's friend," says George. "You're
nice to him and he likes you." He offers me one hundred dollars a
week — an immense fortune!

Back to Venice — I tell Jim about my bizarre job. He raises his
eyebrows, grinning. "Too much, man."

Jim is quiet and introspective. I don't want to trespass on his
emotional territory when it comes to Mary, but I'm surprised that,
other than asking how she's doing, he doesn't probe.

I spend my first "work" week hanging around with Hunt,
often in the back of the Rolls as he incessantly activates his foolish
siren, my eyes flicking over to see gentleman George's pained face
in the rear-view mirror.

One day, after lunch, we drive up to Beverly Hills to the enormous estate that belongs to Hunt's father. The driveway leads to
an imposing stone gate, but we don't go in. The place has an abandoned look and feel to it, and the weeds need yanking. George
informs me that he is an employee of one of the wealthiest and
best-known men in the U.S. and that one of his responsibilities is
to take care of the son.

The first week is challenging, but at the end of the week George peels off one hundred dollars from a wad of bills. I head straight to Venice and find Jim. "We're rich, Jim!" We head over to Main Street to stock up on the necessities of life: food, beer, smokes.

"What about your *LA Times* job, man?"

"They're flexible, and I don't know how long this Hunt gig will last — if I even want it to."

A short while later, I tell George that, even though I like Hunt, I prefer making money at my flexible *LA Times* job. George and I amicably agree to end the arrangement. Beach bum life was far more appealing than a full-time job. The *LA Times* took care of the bare essentials, including some room and board.

Content and carefree on a lazy California day, Jim fires up a joint. We stroll along the beach in a haze. We've eaten, we have beer, and we've got cash. Life is sweet.

7: **bloodbath in venice**

Homeless had a different meaning in 1965. It meant that you didn't have a home at the moment — it seldom meant that you didn't have a place to sleep. Homeless didn't mean hopeless. There was lots of sharing going on. "Hey, man, you can crash at our place." "You're welcome to sleep on the couch." "My sister has an empty room." "You can sleep in our loft." People were crashing wherever — for a day, a week, a month. It wasn't a big deal.

But Jim preferred his roof. A friend gave him keys and access to the roof of a seedy three-storey apartment building in Venice, half a block from the beach — Jim's private oceanview penthouse, complete with a sleeping bag. I had a couple of sleepovers, but I preferred a roof over my head, not under it. I remember being stoned, gazing up at the stars in awe, though, as we talked into the night. It had none of the comforts of home, but Jim seemed right at home there.

Some days were leaner than others. Occasionally, the odd tinge of hunger — never starving, but there was never steak on the menu. Jim ate a lot of canned beans and his caretaker friend provided some meals. I always had at least a bit of money, but it had to last until Friday, my *LA Times* payday. On one of those lean days, Jim found some quarters in the grass, and we shared a hot dog and a Coke. We were both slim — two 135-pound guys with long hair. But we had a sense that things would work out somehow. We were living in the moment.

Jim didn't talk about any friends, and I wondered if he compartmentalized his life. He seemed lonely. It was always just Mary and Jim at her apartment. He only ever mentioned the friend who gave him access to the roof he slept on, a guy from film school, but I never met him.

We got to casually know others living the bohemian/hippie lifestyle. They lived in rundown rooms or bungalows in the alleys of Venice, or in neglected cottages on the fouled canals. There was always a place to crash and share a joint. Still, Jim preferred the roof, where he could be alone, have a joint, drop acid, and write. He was always writing.

We smoke grass and sashay through the days, sitting for hours, with long periods of comfortable silence, watching people, ocean-gazing. Curiously, dope is always available; there are lots of kindred souls here. Today is where it's at.

Another pristine day on Venice Beach. Marijuana magnifies the warm caress of the ocean breeze, this flowing calm. I wonder how long I can spend in marijuana's embrace — Jim has opted for 24/7. Sitting on the beach with our backs against a palm tree, gazing at the sea. This glacial pace — *is life really this ... slow?* Another day of quiet bliss.

Jim and I are talking about sex. How he was a virgin until he and Mary had sex, and how it wasn't that great because of Mary's Catholic upbringing. Since he has been involuntarily single, his sex life is heating up. Looking at him, I think, *no wonder girls are attracted to him.* He looks great with his sinewy body, lovely eyes, handsome face, and long, curly hair. The tan is a finishing touch.

He asks me about my experience with girls.

I had spent years with my sisters and mother after my dad left us at a young age. My brother always seemed to be at our grandparents'. It gave me a female perspective. "I think girls sense that I genuinely like them, which I do. I understand girls more than most guys," I tell Jim. "Although I really get along with girls, I can count my sexual experiences on one hand."

"Interesting," Jim muses, looking out to sea. "The way the female experiences sex is so different than the male. I would like to meet a girl who is completely un-hung up about her sexuality. Open, free, no limitations."

The rhythm of the waves is hypnotic. They rear up, suspended, like they're holding their breath. I see them cascade, a soundless gap, then slamming onto the beach, the crash strangely muffled.

"Hey, how're you doing?" Jim says to a dazzling girl gliding by. She pauses, looks down at us. "Okay. And you?"

"Want a toke?" says Jim.

She remains standing, indifferent. He reaches up, passes her the joint. Venice is home to a mixed bag of peaceniks, bohemians, dropouts, runaways, and hippies, but there are crazy people to be avoided. She sizes us up for a minute, then sits down beside us.

"I'm Jim, this is Billy."

"Hi. I'm Leslie."

Three people at ease, bums warmed by the sand. Idle chatter turns philosophical, the conversation flowing. We're talking about the rhythm of the waves, the rhythm of life, the rhythm of the planets. Discussing nature, evolution, consciousness, the cycle of life. In the midst of this, Jim quotes a line: "We eat — and we are eaten." She looks at him, puzzled. I've grown accustomed to the zigs and zags of his mind.

In late afternoon, the sun's angled rays bombard the surface of the ocean, creating a billion sparkles. I look into the girl's eyes. Same sparkles — the white in brilliant contrast to the liquid brown iris of her eyes. Eyes framed by impossibly long black lashes. I'm wondering how such deep, enchanting eyes without an apparent trace of makeup could be so beautiful and animated. I am amazed at her femininity. Good Lord, is this beauty real? Or weed-enhanced? She is living art.

I'm not shy, but Jim is painfully so. We have little to offer, other than our company. We have very little money, are essentially homeless, but we are kind and authentic. And we can engage. "Do you want to stroll with us?" invites Jim.

I notice her deep tan against her white lace peasant skirt that sways as she moves along the sand; her hair glowing in the sunlight, her skin flawless. "I'm thirsty. Are you guys?"

Cold beer on a hot day. Life is beautiful.

Leslie enchants us. Jim awkwardly smiles at her. I awkwardly smile at her. She's lovely. It's a long weekend, although every day is a long weekend. As the sun shimmers on the horizon, Leslie tells us that she's a teacher.

"What do you teach?" Jim asks.

"Literature."

One of his favourite topics; the conversation accelerates.

"Are you guys hungry? I know a cheap food joint on Main Street."

Three blocks off the beach, we order a combo and more beer, then amble back to the boardwalk, toward Venice Pier. The beach is empty. Jim lights up a joint. We are floating along under a cloudless night. Talk about this, chat about that. "Wow, can you smell the salt air?" "Can you see Aquarius?" "Is that the North Star?" "No, man, the brightest star isn't the North Star, it's Sirius."

How come he knows so much?

We have become a happy, harmonious trio.

"Do you guys want to come up to my place for a glass of wine?"

Hell yes!

Up the elevator we go to her apartment on the fifth floor. It's clean, with nice furniture, the cream-coloured living room couch facing the ocean.

Out on the balcony, Jim and I take in a breathtaking view of Santa Monica Bay. From Palos Verdes on the southern tip to Point Dume in Malibu; the broad beach from Venice Pier to Santa Monica Pier — our territory.

Some wine. A mesmerizing girl. Maybe a place to crash. Our fortune is turning — the night before it was a sand mattress under the pier. She pours glasses of wine, a luxury item. Easy conversation, glasses drained, she pours us more.

"So, you're from Canada, Billy? Are you in university?"

"Not anymore," I say. "Issues with the dean."

"He's a rebel." Jim laughs.

"What about you, Jim, what do you do?"

"I write."

"What kind of writing?"

"Poetry mostly, and, you know, things I think about."

"Do you make any money at this?"

"Nope." Jim rolls another joint.

"Are we in a movie?" I say to Jim when she goes to the bathroom. He sits there grinning.

Now we're sailing, too many sheets to the wind. Jim asks, "Do you have any acid?"

"No," says Leslie, "I only have grass."

"Do you have any diet pills?"

Puzzled, she goes into the bathroom and brings out a bottle of yellow pills. Jim downs a few, then pours some into his hand. "Come on, have some!"

Leslie and I hesitate, then ... "What the hell, why not?"

The world starts turning … *weird*. Thoughts gallop through my mind too fast to snare. Jim's eyes are restless. I look at Leslie, her eyes dancing.

Jim and I are back out on the balcony again, staring at the ocean. It is awe-inspiring. Silver moonlight shining on the ink-black water; the quiet wash of waves meeting the shore. "Hey, let's go for a midnight swim," Jim says, impetuously whipping off all of his clothes, turning to Leslie. "Come on, girl, lose your inhibitions." He turns to me. "Come on, man, take off your clothes! Let's go skinny dipping!"

Just like that, we're all naked, running down the hall, laughing like mischievous kids. Nobody is on the elevator. We dash across the deserted lobby to the beach and splash into the sea. Holding hands to steady ourselves against the mild strength of the waves, the ocean washes over us. Emboldened, we plunge into the pitch black. Gliding through the frothy water, we are free; we are stoned, ecstatic. Three free spirits on a midnight swim.

Now, about seventy-five feet out in the ocean, I look back at the shore and see the apartment lights reflected in the ocean mirror. Where are Jim and Leslie? A wave nudges me, then another. I'm floating, at peace, until … *Jesus, what the hell is that?!* Something long glides along my leg. Panicked, I yell out and see Jim's grinning face bobbing between the waves. "Hey, Jim, something weird just happened." I describe it. His eyes widen. "Let's get out of here!" and he motions to Leslie. We emerge from the water, run up the sand, across the lobby, and into the elevator, nude and dripping.

Back in the apartment, Jim pours more wine, pops more pills. "Let's have a hot bath," he says. He's getting stoned — and really drunk. Leslie has lots of wine, something we couldn't afford.

"Great idea."

I fill her bathtub with water, and the three of us, chilled to the bone, gratefully sink into the water's warm embrace, Leslie in the middle.

"We need some bubble bath," says Jim.

"I don't have any," says Leslie.

I get out of the tub, search her cupboard and find a bottle of perfume — a brand new bottle of Estée Lauder. I wrestle with the top. "I can't open it," I say as I ease back into the tub.

"Hey, man, pass it to me," says Jim.

It's sealed too tight. The top won't budge. Jim holds the perfume bottle in his open hand and slams it against the side of the iron tub. There's a crack in the bottle. The room floods with a powerful, overwhelming scent. Jim immerses his hand in the water. There is a trickle of red, and we watch transfixed as it slowly spreads, weaving between us. His blood.

"Too much, man," he says. "We're having a bloodbath."

The lights are out, candle flames flicker, the mirror reflecting strange shadows. Jim slowly weaves his hand back and forth in the warm water, creating a scarlet current that swirls around our slippery bodies.

Leslie eases herself out of the tub. Her body glistens in the last flicker of the candles. Her tan lines give the illusion that she is wearing a white bikini. Jim and I are in the tub as she turns to face us. She is stunning, wrapping a white towel around her head. A goddess.

"I feel like lying down," she says as she strolls into the living room. Jim glances at me, raises an eyebrow. She's at the fridge pouring wine none of us need. She hands us each a glass and moves into her bedroom. We follow. Snow-white sheets accent her bronzed body. Jim crawls onto the bed to the right of her, me on her left. We lie on our backs. I can hear the sound of the waves through the open balcony door. I feel her light touch on my leg. I turn my face toward her. Jim is caressing her. Laid-back, no urgency. A slow mood shift. Passion building. I touch her silky skin, the scent of luxuriant damp hair. And Estée Lauder. Jim embraces her. She is moving against him, but nothing is happening. "What's wrong, Jim?" she asks.

"I, ah, don't know. I'm, ah, pretty stoned." Jim crawls over us and stumbles into the living room. We hear the clink of a bottle against a glass.

Her face an inch from mine, Leslie turns to me and whispers. She moves onto me. Fifteen minutes later, Jim staggers back into bed. We are drifting off. The last thing I hear is the soothing sound of the waves washing on the shore. We are at peace.

We wake up with horrible hangovers in too-bright daylight. Leslie in a white fluffy robe. The heavenly aroma of fresh coffee brewing. The three of us stumble around, feeling awkward, but not for long. Jim fires up the first joint of the day and steps out onto the balcony. He's looking down at a commotion on the beach. Some official trucks, a crowd talking to uniformed men.

"I wonder what's going on down there, man."

We join him on the balcony. Jim steps back inside, puts on his T-shirt and blue jeans, runs his hand through his mane. "I'll be right back. See what's happening."

Leslie and I leaning on the balcony rail, watch Jim languidly stroll toward the crowd. He's talking to some excited people gesturing toward the ocean. Jim looks out to sea, then shifts his gaze up to us. Shaking his head, he turns and heads into the building.

Back in the apartment, his face is animated. "You won't believe this, man. That crew was there because they had to deal with a shark that got stranded between the sandbar and the beach last night. We were swimming with a shark!" He's exhilarated. "Amazing, man!" The danger excites him. He fires up a joint, passes it to Leslie. "Let's have some wine."

———

Next morning we say goodbye to Leslie. She heads to school, we head for the beach.

"She's a cool chick, man," says Jim. "I'd like to see her again."

Over the next while Jim would periodically buzz Leslie's intercom and, if she answered, crash at her place. We spent a few serene days on the beach with her and wondered why this cool girl didn't have a boyfriend. Then one night Jim buzzed her, and she told him over the intercom that she had a boyfriend and that she didn't want him to buzz her anymore. He told me this story when we were sitting on the beach smoking a joint.

"So you had a buzz on when she told you to buzz off?"

"Not your wittiest line, man." He glances at me. "You're a smart guy, Billy. You should seriously think about going back to school, man. Getting your degree."

"Well, I sure as hell won't be going back to Loyola for it."

"So, give me the details, man. What went down at Loyola?"

"It's a long story, Jim."

"We've got all day, man," he says. "Lay it on me."

8: california, here i come

"You and Mary had been out here for a while," I tell him. "Meanwhile, I was back in Canada at college in Montreal."

I tell Jim about Loyola, a Catholic Jesuit college, rigid and uncompromising. The dean of residence enforcing unbendable rules: strict curfews, no drinking, lights out, no female visitors. Treating college students like children.

"But Montreal was pretty exciting," I tell Jim.

I described the Ritz-Carlton basement bar, always jammed with McGill University students. The cheap and plentiful beer, jukebox blaring the Beatles, the Beach Boys, the Rolling Stones.

I was settling in academically, but the atmosphere at Loyola was oppressive. I arranged dorm assemblies and called floor meetings to protest the harsh rules and lack of freedom. I had become the dean's nemesis.

In November I wandered into the Royal Bank just off campus to enquire about my student loan. The assistant manager congratulated me. "You have been approved for a five-hundred-dollar education loan." He shook my hand like I'd won a lottery. "Shall I make that payable to Loyola College?" he asked.

I straightened up. "Um, what other choices are there?"

"Well, we can give you a draft …" he said, hesitating, "or cash."

"Um, the cash will be fine."

Jim laughs as I describe how I swaggered out of the bank with five one-hundred-dollar bills in my pocket.

Almost delirious, I went to fetch my roommate, John. A rich kid from New York who would always pick up the bar tabs for all of us poor students. He must have received unlimited funds from his family.

I had enough common sense to hide three hundred bucks in my desk drawer.

"Hey, John, let's go to the bar," I said to my roomie. He was always game for a drink.

I paid for a taxi to the Ritz. When we got out, John headed toward the basement college bar. "No, John," I told him, "we're going to the swanky lounge in the lobby."

A uniformed doorman swung open the polished brass door for us, gave a subtle bow. "Welcome to the Ritz."

Into the opulent lobby we went, up thick-carpeted stairs into the elegant lounge where we sat on burgundy leather stools at the polished mahogany bar. We nodded at the others, amiably chatting.

The bartender, beaming in a tie and vest: "What'll it be, gentlemen?" We ordered rum and cokes, then decided that doubles would be better. "Certainly, sir."

The place was surprisingly full. Two hours later we were best buddies with our fellow bar mates. "Bartender, I'd like to buy all these people a round. Champagne — whatever they want!"

"Ah, Bill, I think we should be heading out," John advised.

"Okay, but first everyone gets a drink — on me."

I paid the staggering bill, and two drunk college guys exited the Ritz, the doorman wearing the thinnest of smiles. We ended up in a French-speaking after-hours club where we definitely didn't feel welcome. But we ordered beers and asked a couple of French girls to dance.

Menacing guys stood all around, eyeing us. At one point, three of them came over. One, in a thick Québécois accent, told us, "You need to go now."

"We're not finished our beer."

"Yes, you are."

With that, they grabbed us and muscled us out the door, the biggest guy shoving me so hard that I tripped and landed on the curb nose first. Blood spurted like a fountain. The next thing we heard was a siren; gendarmes to the rescue. They took us to the hospital. When I went in to emergency, John disappeared.

I tell Jim about the letter my mother subsequently received from the dean.

LOYOLA COLLEGE
Montreal, Quebec
OFFICE OF THE DEAN OF RESIDENCE
November 8, 1964

Mrs. Claire Cosgrave
215 Old Yonge Street,
Toronto, Ontario

Dear Mrs. Cosgrave,

I have the unhappy task to inform you that your son, William, has become such a problem to himself, to his fellow students, and to the general welfare of the Loyola College Residence that I am sending him home so you might speak to him about several matters of his conduct that need immediate correction.

First, William has a drinking problem. On November 8th I was called at 3:30 a.m. to Queen Elizabeth Hospital, Montreal, where I found your son intoxicated, disoriented, and without memory of what had happened to his $500.00 education bank loan — which he received earlier that day. Fortunately, some of that money was found. But because of his conduct I placed your son on Disciplinary Probation for the rest of the academic year. At his request, you were not informed of this incident.

Add to the above his repeated attempts to create factions against authorities among his fellow students, and you have a picture of the problem your son has created for himself so far this year ... and the year is still rather young.

I would ask that you have a long, serious talk with William about these matters. When he returns, he will remain on probation for the rest of the academic year.

Sincerely hoping for William's welfare,
I remain, Cordially Yours,
D.R. Clark
Dean of Residence

"It seemed like the perfect time to take up Mary's invitation to come to LA," I say to Jim. "So, I hit the road."

Jim loves the story. He likes the drunk and disorderly part but is pissed off by the dean. It's a theme with him — the power imbalance and people abusing their authority. "Power corrupts, Billy, inevitably."

9: **lapd**

We're in a park in Venice at three a.m., and Jim says, "Man, this place is lifeless — like a graveyard."

Venice is asleep. The joint hisses as he sucks in the smoke, embers spark and glow.

"Here, man, have some more." Another toke — my mind already far away, focusing on the stars. I snap back to the present and his voice: "The world has stopped, man. We're all that's left." He grins at me; I grin back. We look around. We are the only signs of life. We laugh at the image of being the only two on the planet.

We're floating away from a house party that began as a casual invitation for a beer when the sun went down. A couple we met on the beach. We go with them to their surprisingly well-preserved cottage on a canal. It could use some makeup, but compared to the neglected places beside them and across the stagnant canal, it's a jewel.

We've been watered and fed. Beer followed by beer and snacks and music amid an intriguing blend of strangers, the whole evening friendly and laid-back. Sharing their joints and beer and acid (which is not yet illegal). On my first LSD trip, I feel as if I'm chewing the music, feeling so certain that I have the answer.

"Hey, Jim, I've got it." I'm excited. Earnest. "It's all about love, man! That's it! It's that simple!"

He grins. I start sharing this amazing insight with everyone. Smiling, glassy-eyed hipsters and hippies. A variety show. Dancing in the cramped living room. A small patio speaker brings the beat outside — weaving bodies glistening in the California night. The guys, taut, tanned, and slim, moving to the beat. The girls, damp, braless, dreamy-eyed, hair long and straight. Everybody stoned.

Jim, normally shy, the courteous Southern man, now fully fuelled, winds his way into the swaying dancers. He is also taut and tanned and slim. His hair is now down to his shoulders. Sweaty, flowing hair, eyes shining — blissful; he looks great. Following him, I join in. We are captives to the pulsating rhythm, bumping into each other, holding each other up. Strangers in the night. Dance till you drop — which we're about to do.

"Come on, Jim, maybe time to go." As if I could judge anything. Polite Jim hunts down the host couple and thanks them. Gives them his charming smile.

It is a stellar night. We've met engaging, interesting people. Life feels effortless. Gliding through Venice, heading for the beach, finding a bench. "What cool people," I say. "Happy as hell in the here and now."

"Freedom. Celebrate the moment.... Man, this place is dead." His match flares as he lights another joint. "One more for the road."

We finish it and abandon the bench. It's three thirty a.m. The muffled sound of waves rolling in. Not a creature is stirring. Jim stops, listening: "I hear a cricket ... in Venice. No way, man."

I hear it, too, along with the muted electric hum of the traffic light as we cross Pacific Boulevard.

"Man, what a night," Jim says. "Good weed and acid. Cool, laid-back people."

We drift across the intersection, hypersensitized, the amplified green light glaring like a too-bright spotlight. Two steps from the curb, the light turns yellow. My mind begins to wander. Mellow and at peace, we turn right at the sidewalk.

CLICK.

We glance at each other. What was that? A white door with lettering swings open — POLICE.

Flash! Blinding red and white lights blast on. We shield our eyes.

"Well, good morning, boys. Your ID, please." Enormous white cop, huge gut, dead eyes, flat smile. He looks at our long hair: "You are boys, aren't you?" Sarcasm drips from sneering lips.

Jim asks, "What's the problem, man. We aren't doing anything."

"Too late, girls, you already have."

My mind is swirling. Danger alert. But Jim is beyond laid-back. "Hey, man, no need for sarcasm."

The cop stiffens, eyes glaring. "You call me *officer*, get it?!"

"Hey, man, be cool, we haven't done anything wrong."

"Listen, you queer, I'm telling you for the last time, you call me *officer*."

The vibe from the cop is a toxic brew — anger, hate, resentment. I'm scared. But Jim's energy shifts, his eyes narrowing into a defiant stare. "Hey, man, leave us alone."

As the cop takes a step toward us, the car lurches as a second giant emerges to stand beside his comrade. My tranquil love vibe has vanished. Two enormous cops with hate in their eyes, menace on their minds, blocking the sidewalk.

"Where were you two, and what are you doing out here at three in the morning?"

"We were at a party, man," Jim says.

"DON'T call me *man!*"

They ask where we live. We give Mary's address.

"We could arrest you two long-haired creeps."

"What for?" Jim asks.

"Crossing against a red light."

"That's bullshit. The light was green."

"Sorry boys, that light was red."

Jim's temperature is rising. My instinct is to appease; I'm on red alert. But Jim chooses to confront them. "You can't arrest us for something that didn't happen."

"We have two witnesses."

Jim looks around. "Who?"

The cop is smirking. "Each other."

"Come on, Billy, let's go."

Jim takes a step forward, but the cop blocks him. There's still no traffic, and the cops have turned their flasher off. Jim goes to move around him and the cop puts his hand on Jim's chest. Jim pushes it away. The cop steps closer, eyes fiery, and grabs Jim's shoulder. Jim's eyes are full of fury; he swipes the arm away. "Oh, I get it. Police brutality time!" He tries to shove past the cop.

"You want to be arrested, you long-haired creep?"

"What for, man?" Jim is losing control, taunting, angry. "I know my rights."

"You long-haired pukes don't have any rights. Call me *man* one more time, and you're under arrest."

"Fuck you, man!"

The cop pulls out his handcuffs. Barks at Jim, "Turn around!"

"No way, man."

"You're under arrest for crossing on a red and resisting an officer."

Jim is now shaking with rage, breathing heavily, nostrils flaring, eyes flashing. "Fuck both of you!"

The cops look at me. There is appeasement in my eyes. "Can't you just let us go home?"

They fling open the back door of the cruiser and order Jim to get in.

Jim doesn't move.

They grab him and try to cuff him. He spins and shrieks. They manhandle him toward the back seat; he's lost control, yelling and kicking. The cops are getting rough. Jim is a wild animal about to be caged. They can't dominate him; he's raging and spitting. A torrent of words spew venom. They punch him. I scream, "Leave him alone! Somebody help!"

Jim is out of control. They punch him again; he punches back wildly. I'm panicked, terrified. Jim has become an active volcano. The bullies have triggered an eruption. I try to grab him. The cop, eyes blazing, jumpy, juiced, his partner still pounding on Jim. "You fuck off right now or you're getting it twice as bad!"

Jim is kicking and screaming. They punch him and slam him into the back seat of the cruiser. There is a Plexiglas divider between the front and back seat. Locked in, confined, screaming and raging, Jim's a savage, trapped animal. His eyes are wild; he's crying with fury.

The car is rocking with Jim thrashing and kicking. The driver, adrenalin pumping, eyes on fire, throws me a look of raw hate and squeals off. I am petrified and can't stop shaking.

I find a pay phone, but my trembling fingers can't put the coin in the slot. *Deep breath — be calm, be calm, be calm, stop shaking.* Through the smeared glass booth I see the soft diffused light of dawn. I'm alone in the twilight zone. Got to help Jim. Is he going insane?

I call Mary. No answer. *Shit. Come on, Mary, please answer the phone. Please.*

Is he hurt? Did they arrest him? Is he at the police station ... or the hospital? Nerves frayed, I'm shaking. I run to a restaurant on Main Street. Early-risers are bent over their coffees, having a smoke. The chirpy waitress behind the counter pouring refills. Pointing to a chrome stool, cracked red-leather seat. Gives me a wink. "Be right with you, hon. Grab that seat."

"Um, could I have change for the pay phone, please?" I'm still trembling.

Fucking coin slot, why is it so narrow?

I phone the nearest hospital.

"No Jim Morrison here."

"How about James Morrison? Or James Douglas Morrison?"

"I'm sorry, we have no one registered by that name."

"How about Emergency?"

"One moment please…. Sorry, no one by that name in Emergency."

Same response from the nearest police station.

Where the hell is he?

I head back to the beach. A thick grey cloud is rolling in off the ocean — the marine layer; Venice's very own London fog. Engulfed in the chilly predawn mist, I head to the only home Jim has — the roof on Westminster Avenue. There are sounds and sights of people stirring, but no sign of Jim. I feel anxious, helpless. I slump against the building. Then I move onto the warming sand and drift off.

———

"Hey, man. Wake up."

My shoulder is gently jostled; I squint up at Jim's face outlined against the blinding morning sun. "Am I glad to see you," I say.

"They were smart enough not to punch my face, but I kept yelling that I'm going to have them charged with assault. They kept driving around deciding what to do with me, then dumped me on the beach."

I'm so relieved, I'm speechless.

"Man, am I hungry," he says.

"Me, too, Jim. I've got some dough. Let's go eat."

Jim was free but bruised and sore. The incident probably cemented his mistrust of authority and fuelled his rage against abuse of power. Ironically, when he became an international rock star, he depended on the police to control frenzied crowds clamouring to get on stage. But it was after he was assaulted backstage by a cop before a concert that he mocked the police on stage, which led to his arrest. The charges were later dropped. When I read the details, I wondered if the backstage assault triggered his memory of the outrage he felt that night in Venice in the summer of '65, when he experienced what it felt like to be a helpless victim of corrupt power ... with no recourse.

10: **i just saw jesus**

I meet a girl on the beach. She's with a young child. Tammy and I hit it off right away. Her little daughter, Maria, plays in the sand with a yellow shovel and matching pail, fully absorbed in her task as her mother chats with me. It turns out that Tammy rents a small two-bedroom apartment a few blocks from the beach. I offer to walk them home.

She's a sweet girl who got pregnant when she was eighteen. Her boyfriend deserted her. Her parents were outraged — not by the boyfriend, but by their daughter's "behaviour." Her parents disowned her but agreed to support her if she moved out of state.

"I lived with my sister and her husband, but I overstayed my welcome, so I took Maria and moved to LA."

I tell her about a girl I knew in a similar situation in Canada. Her father was an esteemed doctor and his wife a "society" woman. Before she began showing, they told everyone that she had developed a rare disorder and was bedridden. They would let her out in the backyard after midnight for some air when all the neighbours were asleep. Her father, a skilled surgeon, ironically did develop a disease. At the pinnacle of his career, he had to quit when his MS advanced. She remembered him secluding himself in the den, curtains closed night and day, feeding live fish to the piranha he kept in his aquarium.

No wonder girls were terrified to have sex, even though they did.

Tammy's neighbour had offered to watch Maria when she was asked out on a date, but when the guy found out about her child, he never called back. "That's happened a few times," she says.

"You're a nice guy. I feel that I can trust you," she tells me the next time I visit her. She's staring at her lap, hands folded; then she looks up at me, her blue eyes two shiny globes. "I'm lonely, Billy. Come over whenever you want."

Which I do. She needs a friend, not a lover. She seems grateful for the company. I like her. And I like little Maria, who likes me back. The owners of a private home have an apartment above their garage, which they rent out. Wood stairs lead up to the kitchen door. The space is small, but clean and private. After hanging out with Jim, I have the option of staying at Tammy's, or wherever. Plus, I can give Mary some privacy.

Tammy and I have a casual, uncomplicated friendship. One night I'm asleep on her couch when something stirs me. I rise up on my elbow to see little Maria in her white nightie, staring out the window. *How long has she been standing there?* I wonder. Bathed in moonlight, she slowly turns her head and looks at me. "I just saw Jesus." Then she walks back into her bedroom.

When I see Jim later that day I tell him the story of Jesus.

"Interesting," he says. "The Christians call that a divine visitation."

11: the third man

"Hey, man, what the hell happened to your face!" Jim is wide-eyed.

I find him sitting under some palms by the boardwalk. "Where've you been, man?" His eyes are curious. "I haven't seen you for like a week. Did someone aim a flamethrower at your face, man?"

"Ever heard of Michael Rennie?"

"Yeah, the movie star, *The Day the Earth Stood Still*, a bunch of other dumb movies."

"Yeah, that's the guy."

"Now in a hit TV show, *The Third Man* ... plays the guy Orson Welles played in the movie. What about him?"

"I've been with him ... and others."

He's incredulous. "Come on, man, for a week? What the hell did you do for a week?"

I start at the beginning.

———

A week earlier:

"Mary, can you drive me to a house up in Brentwood?"

Surprised, she says, "You know somebody in ritzy Brentwood?"

"An old friend of my mom's from Toronto. She disappeared when I was a kid and surfaced here in LA."

Janet had been in touch with my mother and had given her an unlisted phone number, like it was a state secret. I'd carried the state secret with me and had just finally called. To my surprise she'd issued an invitation.

"I'm invited to a small dinner party," I tell Mary.

Janet Moran. Bony face, sharp, chiselled nose. Determined coyote-like eyes — dark, unblinking, unreadable. She looked you in the eye until you looked away: *I dare you....*

She's a walk-in freezer of a woman; I wonder what turned her thermostat down.

Mary and I are in her VW Beetle, careening west along Sunset Boulevard. It's dark as hell. Powerful tree roots have nudged up the asphalt in places. It's unnerving; no shoulders, too many curves, no sidewalks. Mary's eyes are fixed and focused on the road. Cautious but quick and decisive. Those bewitching eyes, always alert.

Her headlights flash onto the Brentwood sign — she signals and turns right. Brentwood, the tony neighbourhood where stars live closer to the stars. Another quick right.

We wind up Tiger Tail Drive. *Christ, is it dark.* Almost at the top. There's the number. The house is blocked from view by trees. Between the house and the trees, an impenetrable row of perfectly manicured shrubs forms a tightly woven wall between the trees and a procession of curtained windows, providing the privacy that Hollywood demands. Until they want publicity, of course.

Janet Moran, one of my mother's carnival of characters, had been a registered nurse when she lived in Toronto. That is, until she discovered there was a profession that she could make a hell of a lot more money at in the comfort of her own home. She became one of Toronto's top bookies. The money rolled in, and Janet moved up — a fabulous home in an exclusive Toronto neighbourhood, the entire house decorated in white, a cold black ceramic panther, two feet long, lounging on the thick white living room broadloom.

Welcome to the big time. "I have arrived."

She had also moved up in her social circle, including some gentlemen from a branch office of the mob — loan-shark division. Greed intruded. She took bigger and bigger bets, miscalculated, borrowed from the sharks, and incurred daily interest no one could pay. In straightforward terms, they told her, pay up or we break your neck. They loaned her more. She couldn't pay. Time to collect. The boys knocked on her fancy black door. The ultimatum: "You've got twenty-four hours. We'll be back tomorrow." Dead serious.

Next day, the doorbell rang — a couple of guys in black suits. No answer. They went around back. Shattered the glass. Broke in the back door. Poof! Janet was no more. Gone without a trace.

That is, until she surfaced several years later in LA.

Mary drops me off at the house in Brentwood. I ring the doorbell at the black double front doors, listening to the chimes as the right-hand door swings open.

Janet: older, too tanned. Thin and wrinkled. Too-white teeth. "Billy!" Eyes crinkled in a welcoming smile, but lights on dim. I hug her bony ribs. Thin lips kiss my cheek.

Inside, candles glow. The smell of cigarettes. A maid brushes past me.

Into the living room. *Christ, everything is white* — walls, ceiling, carpets, sofas, chairs, ottomans, lamps, shades. *What's with Janet and white?*

"Come on in, take a look around. Make yourself at home. We'll be with you in a minute." She disappears.

To the left is a long hall with broadloom carpet. Open double doors reveal a huge bedroom, softly lit. More candles. On my right are a den and a bar. Past that, an enormous dining room, a bevelled black glass table reflecting the candlelight. Straight ahead is a view so captivating my eyes widen. Underwater lights illuminate the turquoise pool. Muted overhead lights reveal lush cushioned chairs and chaises.

Past the pool, at the end of the property, I stand on the manicured lawn, gazing in awe at the enormous lava flow of LA's lights below. Off to my right, the Pacific Ocean stretches to infinity. Above, Vincent's starry night.

I smell cigarette smoke. Janet joins me. Beside her stands a tall, handsome man. "Billy, this is my friend Michael Rennie."

The craggy face is instantly recognizable — a Mount Rushmore face. He has high cheekbones, thick eyebrows, and a prominent nose. He smiles widely as he shakes my hand. In a British accent, he says, "Nice to meet you, Billy." He lights up a smoke and offers me one. The sea, the stars, and a celebrity — all in the first hour.

In the house, Janet slides open the immense glass doors; they silently recede into invisible pockets. Behold! The city of angels. The curved white couches were undoubtedly custom made for Janet.

Michael conveys his warmth and fellowship. But his smile is a little too easy, a little too practised. Eyes crinkle and sparkle. "I'm with you." There's a crack in his sincerity. He has a Ph.D. in acting. But I like him.

Janet lounges in her white, embroidered dress with her bony, tanned legs, a cream stiletto heel dangling loosely on her pedicured foot. She glances down the hall to where a shadow moves toward the living room. "Patty, this is a friend of mine from Toronto, Billy."

What a knockout! She's breathtaking. I'm guessing late twenties. She flashes a smile that lights up the immense white room. She is dazzling. *Is she a movie star?* I wonder.

A black-aproned maid appears with a glittering silver tray of champagne flutes. Straw-coloured champagne all around. The crystal is thinner than a petal. Within minutes, Janet commands, "Gladys, bring more!"

I remember that low, flat cold voice from when I was a kid.

Ten minutes later: "Gladys, more!"

Gladys guides us to the dining room. Janet weaves her way in. What a room! Silvery-white wallpaper reaches up to a domed ceiling. One wall is marble. She's paid an A-list decorator handsomely. A thick glass table dominates the space, with upholstered, overstuffed white dining chairs on each side, and at one end, a larger, cushier version with arms — a salute to male dominance and privilege. Candles glow, reflecting off the glass; shadows flicker on the painted white-and-blue sky that adorns the domed ceiling. At one end of the table are four thick white placemats, sparkling crystal goblets, and shimmering rows of silverware. Janet sits at the head of the table, in the man's chair. Michael is across from me, Patty beside me. Gladys arrives with more champagne, then dinner, and yet more champagne.

It turns out that bewitching Patty is not only an actress but also an heiress to a family fortune — which explains the glittering diamonds that match her sparkling eyes. She is irresistible. Breathtaking, talented, and wealthy. I presume she is Michael's date, although he's a hell of a lot older. But he is also great-looking, talented, wealthy, and … a well-connected celebrity.

Halfway through our meal, Janet lights up a Marlboro and nods at Gladys. Gladys takes her barely-touched plate away.

The champagne high reminds me of my buzz at the Academy Awards. I'm light and cruising. Each candle throws off shimmering spokes. Michael's eyes are glistening — so are Patty's and Janet's. Mine must be, too. Conversation is flowing. We are floating, surfing on a sea of champagne.

Michael, with his carved cheekbones and deep-set eyes, spontaneously delivers lines from a play. Patty's eyes light up, then concentrate. She delivers the next line back. Michael serves another; Patty lobs it back. Michael smiles; the patriarch approves. He switches from Broadway to Stratford, throws out a line. Patty rallies. She's terrific. This is getting good. Janet is smiling drunkenly, the Moët & Chandon working its magic. Lazy bubbles cling to the sides of her never-empty champagne flute. The stem dangles precariously between her bony fingers. Her easy smile, lidded eyes still alert: a tense weasel — watching.

"To each is given, 'ere life has flown ... a stumbling block, or a stepping-stone."

We are now dewy-eyed with a shared love for these words, this brilliant show, this sharing, this intimacy. How fluid Michael's delivery, how compelling Patty's response. Electrical currents snap between them.

"Gladys, more champagne!"

But not for me. The room is whirling, a merry-go-round spinning in my brain. I stumble to the living room couch. My mouth is parched. My eyes try to focus. The fire reduced to embers. Candles barely flickering. I'm down for the count.

My eyes open. Forgetting for a moment where I am. I stand up — dizzy and unsteady. *Someone took off my shoes.*

The plush white carpet feels good. *Where is everybody?* "Janet? Michael? Patty?" No answer. The only lights are coming from the master bedroom. I wander unsteadily down the hall. At the end, those double doors — one still open, emitting a soft, glowing light. I edge toward the light, leaning against the wall for support. In the room, Janet, with a smoke and drink in her hand, looks over at me in slow motion. Then back. She's sitting in a chair at the end of an enormous four-poster bed — her coyote-like eyes fixed on a naked couple writhing on the bed: Michael and Patty having sex.

My first thought is *Wait till Jim hears this.* My second thought: *This is too weird. I shouldn't be seeing this.*

Shocked, mesmerized, and embarrassed, I back out of the bizarre scene, back down the hall. I pad around on the luxurious white broadloom until I find a closed door, hoping it leads to a bedroom. Inside, a large bed with no one in it, fresh flowers on the nightstand. I drop my clothes in a heap and slip between the sheets. Christ, what a night!

The next morning, I awake late, floating in butter-soft sheets and fluffy white pillows. Two nights before I had slept on a tattered couch in a Venice dive. Life.

I wander into the living room and see Gladys serving coffee and pastries. Michael, Patty, and Janet are up, merry as hell.

"Well, well … almost good afternoon!"

Heh, heh, heh. They're acting like last night was … normal. Smiling like nothing happened. Maybe it *is* normal. *To them.*

"You were saying last night that you'd love to get into acting," says Michael.

I did? I'm wondering what else I said.

"Well, if I could actually act, I think I would love it. I've always been interested in what acting is all about. Did I mention that I enrolled at the Mickey Rooney School of Acting?"

Michael chuckles. "Yes, you did, but you had to drop out after two lessons because you couldn't afford it." Chuckling again. "It's just as well."

He continues: "I'd like to help you, so I called my personal agent this morning and asked him to see you and arrange a screen test for you. You've got the looks and personality. I'd like to see you take some proper acting lessons." He gives me his paternal smile of approval.

I'm wide-eyed. "Thank you very much, Michael."

Patty, equally fetching this morning with minimal makeup, flashes her impossibly blue eyes at me. "Welcome to Hollywood!"

"You'll stay for dinner, won't you, Billy?" Janet asks.

She issues the order to Gladys. "A pitcher of martinis."

What the hell's in store?

Through the post-dinner fog, Michael tells me, "I think you've got something — I think my agent will agree."

Hmm ...

Next morning, I'm hungover, shaky from the endless flow of booze. I awake in the same silky sheets. *I could get used to this.* There's no one here, including Janet.

I call the number Michael left. His agent, Cameron, answers: "Yes, Michael told me about you. Can you come in tomorrow at one for a meeting and I'll arrange a screen test?" *Can this be happening to me?* "Michael will give you directions."

I wander onto the sun-drenched terrace and gaze at LA spread out before me, thinking, *The possibilities!* Stripping down to my underwear, I dive into the pool, then ease myself onto the air mattress floating in the water ... and fall asleep.

Over two hours later, I startle awake. And I panic. I can't see! *What the hell? Why can't I open my eyes?* Still floating on the air mattress in the pool, I dip my hands in the water and soak my face. I try to open my eyes. I paddle to the side. Searing sun, windless air. Terrified — splashing water on my eyes over and over — *Christ, I'm blind!* Feeling my way to a chaise, I lie down.

Eventually, the smallest sliver of light squeezes through. I stumble into the house to what has become my bedroom and look in the mirror through my slits. I am crimson-red, scorched, barbecued. My eyes are swollen almost shut. "Janet!" I yell.

Dead silence.

I wait a couple of hours before calling Michael's agent. "I'm terribly sorry, Cameron, but I'm so sunburned ... "

"No problem, Billy. Let's make it for a week tomorrow ... let's see, two p.m. at my office. Maybe Michael can drive you."

Janet comes home. "You've got severe sunburn. You're not going anywhere." She is a surprisingly tender nurse to my swollen face. "Stay here until you're better."

Why wouldn't I? The next few days it's mostly Gladys and me, with Janet coming and going at weird hours.

There's happy chatter poolside. Michael and Patty are back, with Gladys serving the three of them the old standby — Moët on a silver tray. There are big smiles, warm hellos. My skin has turned from crimson to reddish-brown. Nodding approval comes from Michael: "Your colour makes those eyes even bluer! You're all set with Cameron. I've got an appointment, but Patty will drive you."

"Great! Thank you very much!"

I'm looking good for my screen test in two days. *Look out world, here I come.*

The next morning, I'm still at Casa de Janet. One day until my big day.

I check the bathroom mirror. *What the hell's that on my face?*

"They're blisters," says nurse Janet, "and they're going to burst and peel."

Which they do.

The next morning it looks like someone threw napalm in my face. I call Cameron ... again. He's not pleased. "Look, Billy, we're putting off this screen test until you can promise to keep the appointment. I don't care what Michael says."

I see my film career crashing and burning.

Patty is driving to Santa Monica to do some shopping. "Can I get a lift, Patty?"

"Of course," she replies, her earnest eyes smiling.

Her black Mercedes convertible is parked in the driveway. I open the driver's door for her then slide into the passenger seat. Cruising through Brentwood with the top down, a beautiful woman at the wheel, her blond hair blowing in the breeze, white sundress, deep tan.

Patty pulls up to the Santa Monica Pier, leans over, and kisses my cheek. "So nice to meet you, Billy. See you soon!" Staring at my face, a concerned look in her sky-blue eyes. "In the meantime, be careful!"

It's about a two-and-a-half-mile stroll from the Santa Monica Pier to Venice Pier. Within half an hour I find Jim.

"Hey, man, what the hell happened to your face?"

Intrigued, he fires up a joint. I tell him the story, wrapping it up with a Brando imitation: "Jimmy, I coulda been a contender — I coulda been somebody."

Staring at my napalmed face, he lets out a hoot.

I had always thought acting would be fun, that I'd be good at it, that being a star would be cool. I loved the movies. I remembered the rush of acting in the high-school play. When Mary invited me to LA, I admit I harboured a slim hope that something might happen for me. I still remember the thrill the first time I saw the famous HOLLYWOOD sign. But I had to stop my Mickey Rooney lessons: Strike one. Now I had missed a golden opportunity with Michael Rennie: Strike two.

I wanted to be a star but never got close; Jim had no such ambition and became a world-famous rock star.

Life.

12: don't puke in the sink

I can't take the *LA Times* job anymore. The phone numbers that they provide to cold call are yielding a higher success rate, but I discover that they have fine-tuned the call list so that it is almost entirely low income and poor people we are pitching. It turns out that they are more sympathetic and willing to sign up, even though they can't afford it. I tell Mr. C.J. Walters that I'm quitting.

I have saved some money but not enough. It's time to call in a loan. I write to my brother.

Dear Larry,

Things are going great in LA. Jim and Mary have
become my close friends. I love them. They are
the best part. But I'm low on dough. Remember
when you wrote to me from Europe, almost begging me for money, and I sent it?

  Well, LA is becoming my Europe. I need
the two hundred bucks I loaned you. Now that
you're back in Toronto and working, I'm sure you
can help me out. I wouldn't ask you for it back if
I didn't really need it. But I do.

  Here's the address. Thanks!

Love,
Bill

———————

Another seamless day on Venice Beach, and Jim and I are wan-
dering aimlessly. We slide under the pier and roll a joint. Soon
the dope's embrace is shifting our perception, magnifying our
senses. Silent palm trees, the repetition of waves washing onshore,
slow motion breaths of warm summer air. Our world is a tranquil
place. Jim shows me a notebook with some words he has scribbled,
crossed out, rewritten — a poem about crawling into your brain.
"… I mean the game called go insane."

  "What do you think?" he asks.

I read it again. It takes me a long time. The pot has put us in a time shift. Like a 78 record playing on 33. Everything slowed down. Everything mellow.

"I think it's interesting and, um, different," I say.

He shows me more pages of scribbles, erasures, rewrites, cross-outs. Not like any poetry I was forced to read in school. Stream of consciousness — but somehow defined. Narrative poetry. Plus notes, observations, and his thoughts. He's forever writing in a notebook. I wish I were as smart as him. I feel like I'm a younger brother who doesn't quite get it yet. Sentences that obviously make sense to him, I wrestle with.

The slow-motion hours drift on by. The sun is now hovering on the horizon. Tips of rolling waves sparkle like champagne in the final rays.

We run into some casual acquaintances, lean and long-haired like us. They invite us to share a meal in their dilapidated Venice shack. Of course we're in. After downing hot dogs and beans, and some stimulating conversation, it's time to head out. "Thanks, man. See you later."

It's late as we amble back to the beach. Jim and I are on a midnight stroll. We sit by the seashore listening to the waves. The firmament is bright tonight. Few other souls are out here drinking this in. Jim lights up a joint. We lie back and gaze in amazement at the canopy of stars.

"Billions of solar systems in our galaxy, man, and billions of galaxies." Jim stares up, transfixed. "Think of it like this, man. Earth is a grain of sand on an infinite beach."

"I feel so insignificant, like how can I possibly matter?"

"You mean, as in, what's it all about?" He chuckles. "I've read and studied philosophy," he says. "It's fascinating, man. You should get a couple of books."

Lying on the sand, we finish the joint.

"Let's go to Ray and Dorothy's," says Jim.

"Who's that?"

"Ray and I graduated from UCLA together, and I hadn't seen him since. I was walking along the beach the other day and bumped into him out of the blue. You'll like him."

"Great. Where do they live?"

"Not far, maybe ten minutes. He's a musician, a keyboardist. I told him some song ideas I have and showed him my writing. He's excited and thinks that we can make music together. You know, he composes music for my words."

"What kind of music?"

"Rock 'n' roll. He's actually in a blues/rock 'n' roll band."

"Shit, that's great, Jim!"

He's grinning. "Who knows, man."

"Will they be up this late?"

"Ray will be. Maybe not Dorothy. She works."

We walk in easy silence along the beach. Living in the moment, our life is calm, relaxed, laid-back.

Jim knocks on the door. A studious-looking, serious-faced fellow in wire-rimmed glasses welcomes us. "Hey, man, come on in. Who's your friend?"

"This is my friend Billy, from Canada."

"Canada ... cool! You guys are giving our Vietnam draft protesters safe sanctuary," he says. "Nice to meet you, man. Come on in."

We head into the tiny living room and he introduces me to his girlfriend, Dorothy.

Ray rolls a fat joint. It makes the rounds.

What is this? This stuff is actually blowing my mind. Psychedelic images are rolling through my mind. Slow-motion conversation. "Hey, man" this and "Hey, man" that. Lots of talk about film and music, jazz and rock 'n' roll. And Jim's writing.

I like Ray. He's warm, smart, and engaging. He has a serious demeanour, but he is easily enthused. He's unpretentiously cool. Like Jim, he doesn't have a job. He was sitting on the beach watching the waves when Jim ambled by.

Dorothy is quiet and composed. She's an artist with a day job. Like Mary, in a way, except Mary works at night.

I focus on a large framed print hanging on their wall, poster-sized — maybe two feet by two feet. I study it intently for an eternity. I'm absorbed by it. It's the surface of the moon, all crevices and mountains and creases and folds. Fascinated, I finally ask, "What is that, Ray?"

"It's Dorothy's magnified nipple," he says, his expression coolly matter-of-fact.

I awkwardly glance at nonchalant Dorothy.

More grass, more conversation meandering into the night. The last joint takes us over the falls. I'm not going anywhere. Later, I get up, zonked and nauseated. Rushing to the cramped bathroom, I puke in the sink.

=========

The sun is rising. We stir. Somebody lights a joint. *Let the day begin.* Ray takes Jim aside and murmurs something.

I say goodbye, thank Ray and Dorothy, and wander out into another pristine day. As we stroll along the seashore leaving a trail of temporary footprints, Jim puts his arm around my shoulder. "Hey, man, next time you come here, puke in their toilet — the sink is blocked."

As Ray and Jim developed their music, it was Dorothy who supported them. Ray said later that without Dorothy, the Doors would not exist. Jim would accompany them to city hall when they got married two years later — a rock-solid marriage that stayed that way.

13: a kiss to build a dream on

I still can't get accustomed to Jim and Mary being apart. Even after the weekend Jim and I spent with Leslie, it's hard for me to imagine that the dream couple has actually broken up. Guys will be guys and all that — a weekend fling; Jim sowing his wild oats. Mary stubbornly insisting that they are broken up until he figures out what to do with his life, and she with hers.

But they had been inseparable. Have they really broken up? Or is it temporary? What about their plan to get married?

I head back to Mary's apartment for a couple of days. I've still got the keys she gave me the first week I arrived. She isn't home, but there's a letter for me propped on the kitchen table. I recognize my brother's handwriting. I tear it open and find not just a letter but also a money order for two hundred dollars. *Hallelujah!*

Too tired to even think of going to see Mary at her club, I take a warm shower, grab a blanket and pillow, and drift off on the couch.

I wake up to another inevitable sunny, warm California day, brush my teeth, and make some coffee.

Mary emerges from the bathroom with a towel wrapped around her. Christ, she is so attractive — last thing at night and first thing in the morning. She closes her door and appears moments later in jeans and a white blouse. "See you later, Billy," she says. "I have an appointment with my agent."

———————

I spend an aimless day in LA after cashing my money order. Mary comes in a few minutes after I get home: bright smile, happy eyes. "What a great day I had!" she says.

She opens a kitchen cupboard, takes out some grass and papers, and rolls a joint on the countertop, then starts looking around for matches. "Oh, I've got some in my purse." She goes into her bedroom, finds the matches, and lights up. I wander in.

"Want some, Billy?"

I sit beside her on the bed as she passes me the joint. Almost immediately the grass starts to magnify my senses. She looks at me and smiles warmly. It amazes me how Mary can be so intense, yet other times so carefree.

Everything feels soft, uncomplicated, easy.

She continues to look at me and I am fascinated by the microscopic brown flecks in her shiny eyes. I am entranced as I unselfconsciously look deeper, studying them, amazed by them. Her eyes are tunnels, and I'm being swallowed by them.

Everything is unfolding in slow motion. I look at her soft lips. They're so sensual. I hesitantly reach forward and barely touch them.

The only sound is the quiet humming of the fridge ... and my thundering heart. Our eyes lock. I lean toward her and brush my lips against hers. And then again. Our lips touch and linger. We lightly kiss. And kiss again. It feels impossibly intimate. In fact, this feels impossible. *Am I actually kissing my unattainable dream girl?* I touch her face and caress her soft, flawless skin. I stroke her hair and cup the back of her head in my hands. She smells like a dream. Her eyes are now closed, but mine are wide open. Ecstasy.

Ding dong! Ding dong!

Mary bolts up. "Somebody's at the door!"

She stands up, runs her fingers through her hair, and heads for the front door.

A moment later she calls from the hallway, "They were looking for Sandra next door."

Fully clothed, we had nothing more than this innocent, passionate, seemingly eternal kiss.

Afterward, we shifted quickly back to our special friends role and carried on as if it hadn't happened. Was I sorry the doorbell had burst this magical moment, startling us back into our "normal" reality? Yes and no. Our stable, reliable friendship, which I so treasured, definitely would have changed without the interruption. I never dreamed that this could happen. It was impossible. But it did. It did happen. Just that once. A kiss to build a dream on.

14: jfk

"Violence is in America's blood, man."

Jim is talking about America's history of violence. About President Kennedy, and the tragedy of the assassination and how it has permanently scarred the baby boomers. "That jolted us, changed us forever, man," he said. "I've written about it."

"I saw JFK live four days before he was murdered," I tell him. "I've never seen or felt anything like it. The crowd's energy. Now I get charisma. I sort of felt like I loved him."

"Where were you?"

"I went to his speech in Tampa," I say. "I had a seat twenty feet from the podium."

"What? How did you get so close?"

"A Secret Service guy gave it to me."

"What're you talking about, man?"

"You remember what a big deal it was, right? JFK visiting Florida? Huge publicity."

"A lot of students went to Tampa from Florida State U. to see him. I should have gone with them," Jim mused.

"The principal at Clearwater High came on the intercom and announced that if we missed school to go see JFK, we'd be suspended," I tell him.

Jim nods and smiles. "Interesting…. Figures," he says.

"So I went."

November 18, 1963

There had been massive coverage of President Kennedy's upcoming visit to Tampa. Unusually large crowds were expected for JFK, the rock star — young, vibrant, smart, inspiring, good-looking, and witty.

Six thirty a.m. The sun had just risen, and so had I. Who knew so many people would be on the road that early? My thumb out, I got a ride from the mother of a schoolmate, who picked me up in her sleek Buick convertible. I told her I was going to see President Kennedy at a place called Al Lopez Field in Tampa.

"Well, that will be interesting, Billy. Do you have a ticket?"

"Not really."

Lots of people were milling around at Al Lopez. I noticed several serious-looking men wearing black suits, narrow ties, and sunglasses. Looking like Xerox salesmen.

There was no one in the ticket booths or turnstiles. Police officers were talking to the black suits, and I passed through a turnstile and wandered onto the field. Husky workers were putting up rows and rows of chairs on the field; others were securing a ramp against the stage to provide access and unloading a podium from a white truck, followed by curtains, flags, bunting. Drifting over to the stage, I see technicians running electrical cords to the centre of the platform.

"Good morning, how're you doing?"

An electrician looked up from his wires and cables. "Great, thanks. Big day today!" He was grinning.

I looked back at the stadium: more police officers, black suits, and people. "So, President Kennedy will be right on this stage?"

"In about five hours. You're awful early."

"I'm Canadian," I said. "We love JFK. I've only seen him on television."

The podium was being centred on the stage. The black suit supervising saw me looking up in awe at the front of the podium: SEAL OF THE PRESIDENT OF THE UNITED STATES.

I was excited already. "Do you think I could come on stage and touch the podium?"

The electrician was smiling. He looked at the suit. "He's from Canada," he told him. "What do you think?"

Suit checked his watch. Looked at me, nodded okay.

"Come on up, but just for a minute."

As I climbed the ramp onto the stage, a technician was placing a red telephone a few feet from the podium. Whoa! I had read about this after the Cuban Missile Crisis. It was a weird thrill to actually see it. "Is that the hotline to the Kremlin?" I pointed at the phone.

The black suit nodded.

"Can I touch it?"

Amused, he glanced around. "Okay, but then you've got to leave the stage."

"Is President Kennedy driving here?" I asked.

"No. He's coming by helicopter."

"Where will it land?"

"Over there. There's actually three identical Marine One helicopters."

"Three?"

"Two of them are decoys — a security measure. No one knows for sure which one the president is in."

"That's amazing. I really appreciate you letting me up here."

"No problem. Where's your seat?"

"I don't have a ticket or anything like that."

Another smile. "Tell you what. All these chairs are reserved for dignitaries and secret service. If you promise to just sit and don't say anything," he said, pointing, "you can sit over there." What are the chances!

Two hours later, the stadium was filling up. An hour before Kennedy arrived, the place was jammed. I heard a suit saying they had an over-capacity crowd. Some of the women were wearing hats and dresses, the men sports jackets or suits. Others wore shorts and sneakers.

The air was crackling with anticipation. Suddenly, there was a distant clatter and three objects appeared in the sky, getting closer. And noisier. Man, were they loud! Roaring, ear-splitting engines, the blades whipping up the grass and dust. Then the door opened, and there he was coming down the short stairs: JFK in person, trim in a dark suit, a narrow blue tie. Tanned and smiling.

The crowd roared its approval. Walking up the ramp onto the stage he was waving and shaking hands. Behind the podium, he beamed down at the nearest rows. *Did he just grin at me?* That was what thrilled feels like. The excitement in the crowd was like powerful invisible waves rolling toward the stage. JFK in living colour. He seemed so charming and gracious.

After his speech, filled with inspiration and hope, he moved into the enthusiastic crowd, shaking hands, touching people. The suits guided him toward the midnight-blue convertible limousine that had been brought onto the field, Secret Service cars in front and behind. Surrounded by the suits, the president boarded the convertible and was driven out of the stadium, waving at the ecstatic crowd. Those people adored this man.

Four days later, an assassin's bullet shattered his skull, splattering his blood and bits of his brain on to Jackie's pink suit. John Kennedy was dead; this young beacon of hope and inspiration, murdered in the same convertible that whisked him out of Lopez Field four days earlier.

The nation and the world were united in shock and grief, with many inconsolably weeping in public or in private. Two days later, tens of millions of grieving Americans, already shell-shocked and glued to their televisions, witnessed the first human killing on live television. Lee Harvey Oswald, the man who murdered President Kennedy, was shot in the basement of the Dallas police station by Jack Ruby in front of dozens of reporters. This was the beginning of the end of innocence. The first network to interrupt regular broadcasting with the news bulletin was airing a soap opera, *As the World Turns*.

This is the violence Jim saw in America. Even in sunny LA.

15: the watts riots

It's August, and the city is scalding. LA is begging for mercy. Pedestrians are scowling, their foreheads slick with sweat, shirts unbuttoned, stains spreading under their arms. Matted hair is glued to their necks, tamping down against their skulls. Short-tempered drivers glare at the fortunate few with air conditioning as the blast of furnace heat blows into their open car windows. Record-breaking temperatures have LA on a short fuse.

Watts, a predominately black neighbourhood, exploded last night. It started with a cop trying to arrest a black motorist. The long-simmering volcano of relentless discrimination and exploitation finally erupted into a riot. Stores and businesses were ignited by rampaging mobs, soot-blackened smoke spreading ominously over Watts like a giant shroud. Arson, looting, shooting, killing.

The next day, Friday the 13th, I'm hitchhiking in the skin-melting heat to Venice to meet Jim. Firefighters have smothered the raging fires, but I can still see and smell the smoke. A massive police presence has subdued the mobs. A tension-filled calm prevails. As seen on TV. But hundreds are being randomly arrested, hurling fuel on the fire. Watts is trembling.

Christ is it hot. My T-shirt is glued to my chest, damp jeans stuck to my legs. Thumb out. I'm looking forward to seeing Jim, cooling off in the ocean.

A shiny Cadillac swerves to the curb, jerks to a halt. The back door swings open as I lope toward the car.

An excited voice says, "Hop in, man!"

"Thanks!" I say to the huge black dude in the back seat. He's got a grin a mile wide.

I pull the door closed as the driver floors it. Just like in the movies, the tires squeal then shriek as the car lunges onto the road too fast, right into the oncoming lane. The driver yanks the steering wheel and over-corrects.

"Holy shit!" bellows the giant beside me. The two guys in the front are laughing, whooping it up. These were three excited guys.

"What's your name, dude?" one asks.

"Billy."

"How you doin', Billy. I'm Zeke." Smiling, eyes shining, he shakes my hand — it was like gripping a boxing glove.

The guy up front in the passenger seat swivels, reaches his arm back, shakes my hand, also. He's glowing, too. "I'm Bobby, man. How're you doin'?" Another set of gleaming eyes, huge grin to match. The driver is looking at me in the rear-view mirror with a third pair of flashing happy eyes. A carful of bliss.

What the hell are these guys on? I thought.

"I like your car," I say.

They look at each other. "It's not ours, man. We stole it."

"Excellent choice with the air con option," I say.

That's a knee-slapper.

"Where you headed, man?"

"Venice, to see a friend. "

"Where you from?"

"Canada."

"Canada's cool. You want to come to a party before you go to Venice?"

"Um … sure." These boys are blissed out, agreeable and friendly. "What are you guys on? Whatever it is, I want some."

There are guffaws all around. "Vodka, man, vodka. We got enough for a lifetime, maybe two!" More hoots. They pass me a bottle, still half full. "Have some!"

"Where's the party?"

"Zeke's place. We'll be there in twenty minutes."

These guys are a few years older than me, good-natured, and in a very festive mood. They seem like good guys.

"So, dude, you're from Canada? What part?"

"I'm from Toronto. You know where Detroit is?"

"Yeah, man, Motown!"

"Well, Toronto is a few hours' drive from Detroit."

"Cool, man."

"What's your president's name?" asks my friend in the back seat.

"We don't have a president; we have a prime minister."

"Whatever, man!"

More big laughs. More big swigs. Their exuberance is contagious. I'm looking forward to their party, to see what's going on, meet some new people. It's all good, not a hint of malice, at least not in the car.

Suddenly, there's the sound of shrieking sirens. A cop car pulls in behind us, closing in fast.

"Cool it!" Zeke yells to the driver.

But the cop blasts past, then another. Then more screaming cop cars.

What the hell?

"What's going on, you guys?"

"Man, you know there was a riot last night in Watts? Looting and shit? That's where we got our vodka."

"Seriously?"

"Right on, man. Everything was free once the store windows was busted. But it got all crazy. They brought in the National Guard to help the cops. Get things under control."

There's smoke ahead, more sirens, fire engines. The guys are pumped up, excited. Crowds have gathered, hanging around;

armed cops and soldiers line the streets, directing traffic, keeping an uneasy peace. The guarded watching the guards.

Jagged pieces of shop windows carpet the sidewalks. Shattered windshield glass sparkles on the streets like diamonds. These dudes are driving into the bowels of Watts. *Christ, it looks like a war zone.*

"Where are you guys taking me?" I take a big swig of vodka.

"It's cool, man. You're with us. Zeke's house is safe. Wait'll we show you what we got."

In spite of the shotgun-bearing cops, smouldering smoke, and the tension in the air, these guys are in a celebratory mood. I see a bus on its side, windows kicked out. Cars are overturned, skeletons of incinerated stores. The aftermath of frustration and racial rage. Fascinated, I slink lower in my seat as they drive slowly down streets farther away from the threatening crowds and menacing police. Finally, we cruise down an alley in a surprisingly quiet neighbourhood and park at a small 1940s green bungalow in need of paint, its brown lawn in need of water. Zeke's house.

"Come on in, man!" They're giddy.

They lead me through a living room and into a bedroom that is jammed with cases of vodka. They're stacked from ceiling to floor, back to front. These guys are like kids in a free candy store — they never dreamed they could have such bounty. They're rich! And they're sharing. Zeke's throwing a party.

The first guests arrive. We're safe so many blocks from the chaos, but they're pumped up, wide-eyed, on edge. It's their first riot. The jittery tension is palpable. The ninety-two-degree heat has everybody sweating.

More edgy people are streaming in. Adrenalin is pumping. Fiery eyes lock onto mine. "What the fuck's with Whitey?"

"He's cool, man. Don't mess with him, he's Zeke's guest — from Canada."

Zeke, the quiet giant with a hint of menace, rules the roost. Tells one of them to bust open another case of vodka. There is a gleeful frenzy. Like the riot is a giant party. More come in with shit-eating grins and boxes of stolen food — pizzas, bread, milk, chips — followed by cases of beer, Coca Cola, and ginger ale. People are laughing like hell, like they just won the lottery. Whoopee!

Zeke has a beat-up piano in the small dining room. A few keys are missing, but it works. A skinny guy sits down and starts knocking out some R&B; Zeke produces a guitar, hands it to one of the guys. Soon another brother gets up and starts singing.

Two guys and a girl appear. They've got an enormous bag of weed. Now they've got some of Zeke's vodka. The house is getting crowded — and stoned. Another dude arrives carrying a case. Somebody hands him a glass of vodka; he opens his case and hauls out his bass guitar. More people keep piling in.

Live music — the place is hopping and thumping. A girl joins in with the guy singing and I'm entranced. I've never been to a party like this. Such spontaneity and raw talent.

The vodka flows like a river. The air is thick with weed. The blast of all blasts. Live music, live voices, live dancing with a group of people jammed into the sweltering room. Everybody's flying.

A girl grabs my arm. "Come on, Whitey, let's dance." I'm up and jiving, laughing with my partner. Dancers bumping into dancers, music pounding. I'm swimming in a sea of white grins, glowing eyes, steaming sweat. Energy is crackling like lightning. I'm the only white guy, diving headfirst into this intoxicating scene.

A dude takes the bass guitar and slows down the beat. The new guy on the piano puts out some hypnotizing blues, rhythm guitar playing background. Piano man starts to sing and it's mesmerizing. I'm enthralled. I love these people and their spontaneity ... and talent. More terrific playing, then he launches into "Birth of the Blues." Fully fuelled by vodka and weed, I stand beside him at the bench and join in. I'm in the zone. Someone yells, "You've got it, brother!" Emboldened, I sing louder, close my eyes, and let it go. The piano player has stopped singing. I'm solo and I'm nailing the song. I'm in the moment as I belt it out. Somebody is slapping my back. I open my eyes and these fired-up people are clapping and happy: "Give us more of that shit, man!"

Who knew Zeke's white Canadian brother could sing. Now the scene is in overdrive. The heat is on, and it's cooking. The band is jamming, and loud. Crammed in the living room, we've become one pulsating organism, arms flailing, feet flying, hips shaking. Everyone is unified. This is ecstasy. Why isn't Jim here! Immersed in the moment. Inhibitions gone. This rocket has launched and we're all taking off. The frothing crowd is almost out of their minds, entering an altered state.

Man, Jim would love this. Breaking through to the other side.

People have come in with news of another riot happening on Normandie Avenue — more looting, rock throwing, and shooting. They're beating white people up, shooting at cops. The cops are shooting back. Buildings are on fire. Burn, baby, burn. The black people are pissed off, enraged, steaming with resentment. There are thousands more National Guards patrolling, backing up the cops.

Saturday morning, people are crashed on the sofa, the carpet, the beds. An early-riser has mixed quarts of vodka with a splash of orange juice. Good morning, America.

"Hey, Zeke, I've got to get out of here. My pal was expecting me yesterday."

"You out of your fuckin' mind, man? You aren't gettin' out of my sight, and I'm not leavin' my house. There's a riot goin' down, some of the brothers are goin' crazy, beatin' up whites, shooting people. You leave here, you'll be killed. Here, have some juice, settle you down."

I have a drink. So does everybody else. Fat joints are rolled and passed around. By noon, everyone is either stoned or drunk or both. Nobody hassles Zeke's Canadian brother, the token white. "Hey, brother!" Talking to them for hours. Good people, friendly and warm. Gregarious. Generous. Had experienced an assfull of racism, discrimination, and living poor. Way more than an assfull.

Saturday night, people are coming in to report the arrests of uncles and sisters, brothers and fathers. Things are tense, the temperature's rising. I step outside. In the dark the eerie scream of sirens is terrifying. People are getting shot and killed. There's a stronger smell of smoke; the distant crack and pop of gunfire.

Somebody dashes in to report out-of-control rioting — and the arrival of even more National Guard reinforcements. We're not going anywhere. They've imposed a curfew. Leave your home and you'll be arrested ... or shot. I'm trapped at Zeke's.

In spite of the descent into hell in the centre of Watts, Zeke's nonstop party fuelled by the endless flow of free booze — and weed — continues. As does the music and dancing. It's a potent mix of elation and fear as the party careens into the night.

By Sunday noon, the word is out — the riot has been quelled — again. People are dead — a child, police, citizens, firefighters. Over a thousand arrested, two hundred buildings destroyed. But they have restored order. The curfew is lifted; you're allowed to leave your house. Some streets are blocked, and auto traffic is restricted and directed by either cops or the military, who mean business. Signs have been erected to tell you which way to go. One of them states: TURN LEFT OR GET SHOT.

"Hey, Zeke, now I've really got to go, man. My friend will be wondering where I am."

He arranges for one of his guys to drive me.

"Thanks for all you've done for me, Zeke, including probably saving my life. You're a good man. I hope we'll cross paths again — under different circumstances. By the way, great party!"

"Take care of yourself, brother. Maybe see you up there in Canada one day."

He walks me to the car, shakes my hand. I get in the front seat, window rolled down. Zeke pauses, reaches through the window, and his huge hand squeezes my slim shoulder. "Stay cool."

"Where to, dude?" says the driver.

"Santa Monica, if that's okay. To the pier."

"No problem, my man."

———

I'm amazed at how normal everything seems here at the pier —
locals mixing with tourists, eating cotton candy and popcorn, light
banter and laughter. Kids riding the merry-go-round.

I walk along the beach toward Venice, searching for Jim. It
is incomprehensible that people are lazing casually on the sand,
sunbathing, carefree, while twelve miles away lies the Watts war
zone. *Huh?*

I don't see Jim on the beach. Or any black people. I try to picture Zeke and his friends on a blanket spread on the beach, their
vodka in a cooler. Not likely. So much for the Civil Rights Act
passed last year. Jim must be at Ray and Dorothy's place.

I head there and knock. Jim opens the door. "Where've you
been, man? You were going to be here on Friday. All that bad stuff
going down in Watts. Where the hell did you disappear to, man?"

"Watts," I say.

He looks at me. "Since Friday?"

"Uh-huh."

"No shit."

"No shit."

"What were you doing, man?"

"Partying. You would have loved it, Jim."

He takes my arm. "Come on, man, we're going for a beer."

When the riots ended (local residents of Watts called it the Watts Rebellion), thirty-four people were dead, a thousand injured, four thousand arrested, and six hundred buildings had been destroyed.

16: **hollywood palace**

I'd seen the hugely popular *Hollywood Palace* show on television. The Rolling Stones had made their American debut on the Palace stage eight months earlier — twenty million viewers on Saturday night. A different star hosted each week — Tony Bennett, Frank Sinatra, Dean Martin, Judy Garland, Diana Ross, etc.

I decide to take a look and hitchhike from Mary's to Hollywood and Vine — the Hollywood Palace just a block farther up. The stern-faced, jowly guard, necktie half strangling him, greying hair, and a paunch, watches over his domain like an imperial guard.

He's keeping a serious eye on the polished glass doors. Standing tall in front of the sign PRIVATE — NO PUBLIC ALLOWED. He looks at me. I smile. "How are you this afternoon?"

"Fine," he says suspiciously.

I look up at the marquee: HOLLYWOOD PALACE — HOME OF THE STARS. THIS WEEK — BING CROSBY. "Is Bing Crosby inside there right now?" I ask.

"Yes."

"For real? What's he doing?"

"Rehearsing."

"Really! Do they ever let people in to watch?"

"Never." He points. "Read the sign."

"Why not?"

"They are strictly closed rehearsals. They want total privacy. No public. No exceptions."

"I'd love to sneak a peek. I'm from Canada."

"Not a chance."

I go back the next day, and the next. And the next.

He loosens up. "Call me Ray."

"You must love your job, Ray."

"Yeah, it's pretty special. I see all the stars — they say hi to me. And the staff are nice."

"Ray, I've never seen a real TV show in my life. Could you take me in and let me just look for a minute?"

A visit with him is part of my daily drifting routine. Hoping.

He hesitates, sighs, and finally relents. "Okay, but just for a minute."

He unlocks the hallowed doors and leads me through the silent lobby, opens the thick red-velvet curtains just enough for me to see. The entire theatre is empty, except for way down at the front row. A man looks to be in command, instructing the crew. Bright lights illuminate the stage. Stage hands shuffle props, a full orchestra sits off to the side, instruments on their laps. Guys with earphones aim their enormous TV cameras with ABC emblazoned on them. Action central. Fascinating!

"Okay, that's it," says Ray. He leads me back outside. We pass the iconic curved glass ticket booth as he escorts me through the exit door. "Thanks a million, Ray, that was great!"

I'm back the next day, and the next, intrigued by the action at the Palace. I have a new hobby. "Ray, if I promise not to say one word, would you let me sit in the back row for a couple of minutes just to watch an actual taping?"

"No."

"Come on, Ray, just for a minute."

"I can't. I'd get in big trouble."

"But no one would ever see me. It's completely dark at the back."

"I'll think about it."

Two days later, he sighs and slips me in. He's a nice man.

I'm invisible — a dark seat in the very last row, a sea of empty seats between me and the front row and the stage. I'm intrigued. He lets me in the next day, and every day after that. He gets a kick out of my enthusiasm and lets me stay till they wrap up for the day. Fantastic live music. Endless rehearsals. A constellation of Hollywood stars. My hobby becomes an obsession.

I've been sleeping mostly at Mary's, and I haven't seen Jim in days. Mary mentions she got together with him yesterday. *Hmmm — what's going on?* I wonder. She broke his heart. Is she mending it now?

"You're hardly ever here, Billy," Mary says. "Do you spend all your time there?"

———

This week's host is Bing Crosby. Rehearsing, phony laugh, same laugh, same joke — four times in a row. *Hmmm, so singers are actors.* It never dawned on me. Bing takes a seat and another man takes his place standing under the hot lights, makeup people doing their thing, camera operators focusing.

What's going on? I wonder.

A half hour later, the man walks up the aisle and notices me in the last row. He nods. "How're you doing?"

I smile. Should I even talk to him?

"Mind if I have a seat out of the spotlight?" he says.

Turns out he's Bing's friend, right-hand man, stand-in, and driver. I remember Bubbles (my mother) telling me that a good friend of hers goes fishing with Bing. They're great pals. I drop the name. "Do you know Lou Chesler?"

He raises his eyebrows. "No kidding! We have for years, how do you know Lou?"

I explain. We settle into a comfortable conversation. The rehearsal is unusually long, with a couple of performers repeatedly flubbing their lines. I've been there for hours. Time to go.

"Well, I better hit the road. Nice to meet you, Harry. Time to hitchhike home."

"You don't have a car?"

"No, I hitchhike."

"You do? Where are you going?"

"Melrose/Normandie area," I say.

He looks down at the stage. "How about I give you a quick lift home — this rehearsal is dragging on and on."

We walk out the front doors to a car parked in a reserved space in front of the Palace. He opens the door of a yacht-sized turquoise Lincoln Continental with Bing's initials monogrammed above the silver door handle. He manoeuvres the yacht into the traffic. I get Harry hopelessly lost. I don't know which exit to take; we go miles out of our way, miss more exits, slide along dark side streets. He's anxious — he's been gone too long. He tells me Bing gets impatient — and has a temper.

"Thanks very much, Harry. You're very kind," I say when he drops me off. "I really appreciate it."

The next day, when I return to the Palace, Ray is trembling with rage, breathing fire in his military-grey uniform, face ready to explode. "You almost got me fired, you son of a bitch!" He makes a menacing move toward me.

I'm eyeing him warily as I back away. "Ray, what the hell's going on here?"

I recognize the man approaching Ray. He's one of the men in charge. Ray, still pissed off, says, "I told this guy to bugger off and never come back." He glares at me: "If you ever show your face around here again, you're going to regret it for the rest of your life!"

"What did he do wrong?" The man looks at me. "What's your name?"

"Billy."

"I recognize you," he says. "Where are you from?"

"Canada."

"I mean, you look vaguely familiar. What are you doing here, Billy?"

I confess that Ray has allowed me to sneak in and sit at the back. I tell him how much I love the Palace, listening, observing, watching, learning. How I find every day fascinating.

The fellow gives me an easy smile. "No business like show business, right, Billy?" Then he turns to Ray. "Ray, from now on he's my guest. He comes and goes when he wants; you always let him in.

"Come with me." He takes me inside and down to the front row. "Sit here from now on, or wherever you want — you're my guest." He shakes my hand. "Nice to meet you, Billy."

I'm here in the inner sanctum. "Places everyone!" And I take my new place a couple of seats from front row centre. No one is allowed in for rehearsals except the stars, the cast, the crew, a few friends … and me. In between scenes the star host of the week sits beside the director.

A week later, I look up to see a heavily made-up woman in a long form-fitting dress being escorted to the first row. She has an aloof and entitled air about her. The crew is fawning. The director stands up: *hug, hug, kiss, kiss*. She glides into the seat beside him and looks at me.

"Miss Crawford, this is Billy."

She turns and gives me a wide, practised smile. What thick eyebrows. She shakes my hand, turns her sculpted face and presents her cheek to me. This close the beige face powder looks like chalk dust. I kiss the cheek. "So nice to meet you," she purrs. As if.

"Billy, say hello to Joanie Sommers."

Joanie's accompanying Miss Crawford because Joan the actress is also the president of Pepsi Cola, and Joanie, a singing star, belts out the joys of Pepsi in their commercials. Joanie is friendly, bubbly, sparkly … real. We start chatting, playing *where are you from?*

"Oh! You're from Canada! I love Canadians," she says. "Miss Crawford, Billy is from Canada."

Miss Crawford's mascara-drenched eyes hold the indifferent gaze of a lizard — "How nice.…"

I notice how large her lips appear. This close I can see how the border of her thin lips have been over-painted with bright red lipstick. They are larger than life. She thinks she is, too. She is this week's guest host.

I am fascinated by everything. By the complexity of producing a TV show. The acting, endless rehearsals, different celebrities and entertainers — Dean Martin, Louis Armstrong, Jimmy Durante (Jimmy again), Judy Garland, Fred Astaire — and a world-famous big band. I'm thrilled seeing some of these famous names between takes. There are a few preposterous egos on and off camera, but most seem very pleasant and agreeable. Just like the rest of us. Sort of.

They are adored and worshipped by their fans, who get to come in to watch the show after the closed rehearsals. The show is taped and shown on Saturday nights.

The director tells the crew, "Sinatra never rehearses."

Sitting in the front row, I snap to attention.

Frank Sinatra! The legend. The Rat Pack. I know most of his songs. He's going to be here in person. Right here on this stage?!

The cast and orchestra rehearse during the week without Sinatra. A stand-in reads his lines.

Finally, the taping. The "billboard girl," who holds the board with the name of the next act, is a little-known starlet by the name of Raquel Welch.

This is a different audience. The women are more elegant, wear more jewellery. The beauty parlours have been busy. There is an anticipatory tension — it feels hot in here. The suspense builds. Someone murmurs, "He's here." There's a commotion behind the black curtain. The audience is on high alert, harnessed lightning in the room. The curtain parts and out comes Mr. Cool — tanned, relaxed, big smile, blue eyes sparkling. The audience sheds their facade. There is frenzied clapping. They act like they're in front of royalty. King Francis.

"Hi, everybody."

He's so confident and at ease, he could be walking out of his bedroom in pyjamas and slippers. But he's in a perfectly tailored tuxedo.

"Ladies and gentlemen, Count Basie," says Frank.

"What?" My head swivels. I didn't even notice. It's the Count Basie band. The Count *and* the Chairman of the Board.

Frank reads the quips, everybody's laughing, beaming approval and adoration. The man is a legend, and he knows it. He already owns the place. WHAM! The blasting brass introduction, and then the voice. No other singer comes even close. "Fly Me to the Moon."

More signature Sinatra songs follow, his voice and phrasing impeccable. He owns the most recognized and beloved voice in the world. Croon a sad song, their mascara starts running. Swing into a powerful big band piece, they're clapping and tapping. They're giddy, they're happy, they're in love. Sinatra knows it.

"Thank you very much, ladies and gentlemen." A big smile, an exaggerated bow, then another. The man disappears backstage.

The Palace empties quickly, the energized crowd anxious to have a drink, to prolong the magic of a moment with Sinatra.

Spellbound, I wander outside. "Goodnight, Ray."

But he never spoke to me again.

It's quiet out here. Traffic is down to a trickle, and I drift around to the side of the theatre. The parking lot is dark and almost deserted. As I lean against the wall, I gaze up at the Hollywood Hills.

Suddenly, I hear a noise. To my left a sliver of light slices into the dark, growing wider as the stage door opens. A man steps out, pauses — a solitary silhouette wearing a hat. Sinatra lights up a smoke, looks around. He sees me and nods. I look at him, smile, and nod back. I watch him stroll to a sky-blue Jaguar. Another celebrity who's way shorter in person. The engine revs. I'm still leaning against the wall as the Jag edges past me and stops, left turn signal blinking. I watch his famous blue eyes flash in the rear-view mirror. A quick glance left and right and he turns onto Vine. He'll be in the living rooms of twenty million people on Saturday night. I watch him disappear into the night. Alone.

When I describe this to Jim, he perks up. "Interesting, man. What was he like? Was his voice the same live?" He asks a bunch of questions. He would call Sinatra his favourite singer. "Sinatra has an amazing voice, man."

17: the show's over

I have been invited by one of the senior Palace people to a party in Beverly Hills on Friday. "We'll go straight from here. You can come with us, Billy."

It is a wonderful evening. Delicious catered food, smooth wine poured into never-empty glasses. Or Scotch, or gin, or whatever your heart desires. Relaxed and chatting with some of the Hollywood Palace people, I'm being introduced to other guests. *After my aborted screen test, maybe I'll have a second chance with some of these movie types*, I think. These garrulous people appear happy and pleased with their abundance. They wear their success well. Everyone seems to have "arrived." Except me.

"And what do you do?"

"Oh, I'm a friend of Joan's."

Fed and fuelled, they eventually start to filter out. Finally, the host and hostess say goodbye to their last lingering guests.

The wife is teetering on her high heels at the enormous glass front door. In fact, many of us have been teetering for quite a while. I'm wondering how I'm going to hitchhike in Beverly Hills at two in the morning.

"Billy, we'd like you to be our house guest. Spend the night."

What a nice couple, not only inviting me to their party, but extending an invitation to stay.

She leads me up the curved carpeted staircase and down a hall to a guest bathroom so large I could live in it. All I would need is laid out on a white marble counter — toothpaste and brush, soap wrapped in fancy gold paper, a stack of thick monogrammed towels. She hands me a luxurious robe. "Here, put this on. Make yourself at home."

I decide to have a shower. *Why not?* Ten minutes later I emerge from the bathroom. She is wearing creamy white silky pyjamas and standing by a hall table, gazing at herself in the mirror above it while smoking a cigarette.

"Here, I'll show you to the bed. Follow me." The silk clings to her body.

She leads me into a grand, dimly lit bedroom with a loveseat and a glowing fireplace. I stand there staring at the fire, feeling a little awkward. *This is for me?*

Not quite.

"Time for bed, Billy." I turn around. Sitting on the edge of the immense bed, she pats the spot beside her. Except that she's not the only one wearing silk pyjamas. So is her husband. He is in the bed, smiling.

What the hell? Now what have I gotten myself into?

Pretending to be calm, I turn around and make a quick beeline for the bathroom. I grab my clothes off of the counter and hastily get dressed. Cautiously, I open the bathroom door and peer out into the hall. No one in sight. I scramble down the stairs and straight out the front, swinging the heavy glass door shut behind me. The driveway leads out to a winding, hilly road. *Man, is it dark out.* I start walking down, knowing that eventually I'll hit Sunset Boulevard.

My head is clearing up, thinking about what went on tonight. On the bright side, I can see the stars. Plus, the air smells fresh and clean. Hearing a car from a distance, I stand under a pale umbrella of light with my thumb out.

Damn. It's a yellow cab squealing to a stop, brake lights casting a red glow into the shadows.

"Thanks for stopping, but I can't afford a taxi."

The driver gives me the once over. "You'll never hitch a ride this time of night," he says. "Hop in and I'll at least get you to Sunset. No charge."

The kindness of strangers.

"What're you doing out here so late?"

"I was at a party and decided to leave."

"What's your name?"

"Billy."

"I'm Harry."

"Nice to meet you. Thank you for stopping."

The sudden squawking of the radio dispatcher startles me. The loud and tinny voice gives him an address. He's got a fare. We reach Sunset and he drops me off.

It takes two more rides to finally get back to the apartment. Mary's bedroom door is closed. Exhausted, I collapse on the couch.

What a night.

There'll be no encore for me at the Hollywood Palace. I had been hoping that it might somehow lead to something — a gopher job, an assistant stagehand, an apprentice, maybe a second chance at a screen test ... something. But this is it. The show's over. The final curtain.

18: **goodbye, la**

A few nights later, I'm standing with my thumb out on Sunset Strip. A white Rolls-Royce glides up silently and eases to a stop. A middle-aged guy sits at the wheel. He is tanned, his blond hair thinning at the front, a tight-lipped smile. He is alone.

"Hop in."

He's drenched in Old Spice. *What's with these people who think if a drop is good, a quart is better?*

My second Rolls. Tan, buttery leather. Discreet interior lights. Soft music. Luxe!

"Thank you for stopping!" I smile at the driver.

At the next stop light he turns his head and looks at me — an unblinking stare from eyes darker than coal. He is smirking. The light turns green. "You've saved me the hassle of cruising Sunset."

I'm confused.

"Do you want to fuck?"

What! What the hell's going on with me? Stunned, I stammer, "No!"

He pulls over, stares straight ahead. "Get out."

A muffled thump as I close the door and watch the Rolls crawl off into the night. I'd been discarded like worthless trash on the side of the road. Like a McDonald's bag. Jesus! How could anyone treat a person like that?

I was overcome by a flood of emotions — humiliation, hurt, rage, confusion.

When I tell Mary what happened, she is disgusted. Her eyes narrow. "Any girl knows how you felt, Billy." Her tone is serious and angry. "Some men are predatory pigs, no matter what their sexual preference. You've seen how they hit on me at Gazzarri's."

I describe the incident to Jim later. "Interesting. Sexual desire is potent, man," he drawls. "The psychology of sex is complex and mysterious."

We go on to discuss how sexual taboos are imposed on societies, especially on girls. But now, with the pill, there's a sexual revolution. Jim is nodding. "Sex without the fear of pregnancy. Free love, man."

The white Rolls-Royce incident remains too jarring to brush off. I can't let it go. And yet again I am running out of money. I had quit the *LA Times*, and I can't get a real job without a social security number. So, I'm scraping by on the money my brother repaid me. Mary is dancing and dating. Jim is living with Ray and Dorothy and working on their music. What the hell am I going to do, with hardly any money left, and no prospects? What the hell am I going to do with my life? I'm still sleeping on couches. Jim is still broke, and I won't ask self-sufficient Mary for a dime. My California dream diary is fraying at the edges.

"I think it's time to go back to Canada. I need to figure out what to do, where to work, where to live. Get something happening," I tell Jim.

"No way. Are you sure, man? Why don't you stay, man. Something will work out."

When I tell Mary, she says, "It's no problem, Billy, you know you can stay as long as you want."

"I know, but I've got to get something happening, and Canada's my home. I'll have better luck getting a job, getting settled."

The *LA Times* to the rescue. In their classified ads I find *Driving to Columbus, Ohio. Share the gas and the driving.* Perfect! I have a good friend going to university in Ohio. I can visit Gary for a couple of days, and then hitchhike the four hundred miles to Toronto. So, I call the number, and a guy tells me that he and a friend want to drive straight through. They're leaving in three days. "We take turns driving, and split the cost of the gas," he says. "You got a driver's licence?"

"I do."

We agree to meet at the Greyhound Bus Depot on Saturday at ten a.m. His name is Stan. "We'll be in a beige '58 Ford," Stan says. "In the parking lot. What's your name again?"

"Billy."

I go to Venice for the last time. To make the familiar walk from Venice Pier to Santa Monica Pier. I notice yet again how, strolling ankle deep along the shore, the only sounds are the breaking waves, and the rush of water as it washes back down the sand. Noticing also how the foam of the retreating water resembles soap suds. I have a final swim in the Pacific and dry off in the sun. Walking back along the boardwalk, the waves are barely audible. Instead, the imposing noise of people talking, walking, laughing. Speakers shouting, dogs barking.

I watch for Tammy and little Maria, to say goodbye. Tammy has let me sleep and shower at her place, and I am indebted to her.

———

On Saturday, Mary and Jim drive me to the bus depot, where it all began.

Jim points. "There's a beige Ford."

One guy is standing beside the open driver's door smoking a cigarette. Another sits in the passenger seat.

Mary says, "Go and check them out before you take your backpack."

I head over to the car. "Stan?"

"Obviously, you're Billy." We shake hands and he points to the passenger seat. "This is Alan."

Both of them have long hair, pleasant faces. Alan has red hair and a full beard to match. "How're you doing?" he says.

Both are in their midtwenties. There's nothing noticeably weird about them.

"I'll just grab my backpack. Be right back."

Stan opens the trunk.

Jim: "It's been so great, man. Here's the deal: whoever gets it happening first calls the other."

Mary: "Have you got enough for food, Billy? It's going to cost more than you think."

"It'll be tight, but I'll make it," I say. I've got my fingers crossed that I've got enough for gas and food.

Mary overrules her fierce principle of self-reliance for herself … and others. "Here's ten dollars, Billy," she says. "But you have to promise to give it back to me the next time I see you."

"That's a promise, Mary."

I love her madly, but I've never told her. Surely, she knows.

The future seems completely uncertain. Will we ever see each other again? My emotions are surging. My eyes are tearing up. I'll never forget them and our amazing times. Their friendship means so much.

Mary, smiling, is blinking away tears. "You be careful out there, Billy."

We share a long, warm embrace.

I turn to Jim. "What a trip, Jim, all of it." I'm feeling disconsolate, am about to cry. Looking at each other, it seems to dawn on us what a bond we have. "I'm going to miss you," I tell him, "and good luck with the music."

He gives me his shy grin for the last time. "Thanks, man. I'm going to miss you, too." We hug and do the male slap-on-the-back thing. "See you in Canada, or back here soon. And yeah, be careful, man."

"I love you two, lots."

Mary beeps the horn as she pulls away. The last thing I see is Jim turning in the passenger seat, smiling, a final wave. A kaleidoscope of images flashes by as I watch the VW until it disappears.

I put my backpack in Stan's trunk.

"We're thinking we'll drive in three-hour rotations. You okay with the third shift?"

In the back seat, I turn and stare out the rear window, the Greyhound sign fading from view. I'm going to miss them terribly. My best friends. Man, do I feel sad. Really, really sad. This hurts.

"Everything good back there?" Stan asks.

No, everything is terrible.

"Everything's fine, thanks, Stan."

19: can you spare a penny?

The car was a gas-guzzler, and almost all of my pathetic last few dollars went to fuel. My last dinner before I was dropped off at the Columbus bus depot the following morning was a Mars bar. The change from that purchase was nine cents.

I remove my backpack and sit on a hard wooden bench, watching the Greyhounds disgorging weary-looking passengers. I'm so hungry. *What the hell am I going to do?*

I've got nine cents to my name — nine lousy cents. *What the fuck?!* I need a different life. But right now I need a dime to call my dear friend Gary. I had been watching a feeble, skin-and-bones old woman sitting on a threadbare blanket with a cup in front of her. Every time a bus pulled in and unloaded passengers, this sweet-faced old woman would glance up at them and, with her toothless grin, say, "If you're having a nice day, can you share it with me?" as she proffered her tin cup. Remarkably, her earnest face yielded results.

"Pardon me, ma'am. I'm really broke and was hoping you could spare a penny."

Her skeletal face looks up at me. Her blind left eye is a milky white. "And what good will a penny do you, son?"

"I've only got nine cents. If you give me a penny, it'll give me a dime to use the pay phone to call my friend who goes to university here."

"Give me your nine cents, sonny."

Her bony, gnarled hand wrapped in paper-thin skin reaches into her cup. She extracts a dime and hands it to me. "Here you go, boy. You look like you need some food. In case you can't connect with your friend ... take this." She reaches into her worn cloth bag and pulls out a grease-stained white paper bag containing a doughnut. "Go ahead, no harm in sharing. It all works out in the end."

I'm feeling so vulnerable, helpless, and sensitive, that tears start streaming down my cheeks.

She takes my hand in hers. "Some things are temporary, son. You'll be just fine."

Remarkably, holding her hand gives me great comfort. Her toothless smile is so sincere and touching — and heartbreaking.

Waiting on a bench outside, I finally spot my friend Gary's black corvette convertible pulling into the parking lot. We are so excited to see each other. Full of bliss, hugging and laughing — a reunion of two best friends. *Wait'll he hears what I've been up to.*

"Hey, Gary, before we leave, can I borrow five bucks?"

He opens his wallet and hands me a fiver. I walk back into the depot and find my friend. I give her the bill, pat her hand. "No harm in sharing. It all works out in the end."

———

I stay with Gary in his apartment for several days. Then I hitchhike the last four hundred miles to Toronto, where I'm reunited with my family. My married sister Sally calls from Calgary, where she moved with her husband. "Billy, you're home!"

She loves Calgary and tells me it's filled with energy and opportunity. "You should come out here, Billy. You'd love it!" she says. "You can stay with us as long as you want."

Within two weeks, I'm boarding a train heading west. Again.

As soon as I arrive at my sister's, I call the only phone number I have for Mary. I'd tried calling the number from Toronto, and the long distance operator still hasn't changed her mind: "This number is no longer in service."

I call LA telephone information and ask for a listing for either Jim or Mary. "I'm sorry, we have no listings for either of those names."

I've got a place to stay, a few bucks, I'm safe, but I can't connect with them. How are they? Are they still in LA? Did they get back together?

Every few months I try again, but to no avail.

20: finding jim

Almost two years later, I still haven't been able to locate Jim or Mary. And there's still no phone listing for either of them.

Me, I've landed solidly on my feet.

I had contacted a friend of my mother's when I arrived in Calgary, an extraordinary man who is CEO of a growing Calgary company. John Burrows changes my life in ways impossible to imagine, and becomes the most important man in it. Incredibly, I have a mentor.

John has given me a job and responsibilities. He has replaced the rudder on a directionless boat and set it on a new course. He helps me, has faith in me, inspires me. The more responsibilities he heaps on me, the more I thrive. He has turned me into an adult. He became a beloved lifelong friend.

I have a salary, an apartment, a car, and I'm also in love. I'd met Terry — a lovely flight attendant — at the Westin jazz bar, and we've become inseparable. She's smart, happy, and affectionate. I love her optimism and joy.

I want to share my good fortune. *Is Jim still broke? Is Mary okay?* I still wonder.

It's been almost two years since we hugged goodbye and I haven't got a clue how to find them. Until …

"WHAT THE HELL!"

I'm walking along the mall in downtown Calgary with my friend John from the office when I freeze. I see Jim! Christ, it really is Jim! He's ten feet away, staring at me from a magazine kiosk.

Jim!

In less than two years he's on the cover of a magazine? I grab the issue. To my colleague, I say, "This, this is my friend I've told you about in LA!"

"Wait a minute," he says. "You know *the* Jim Morrison? No way!"

Reading the article, I'm speechless, gobsmacked. A huge hit single, "Light My Fire," a monster album, *The Doors* — music I've heard on the radio but not paid attention to.

I find out that the album was recorded at Elektra in LA and race back to my office.

"Good afternoon, Elektra Records…."

"Hello, I'm calling long distance for Jim Morrison."

John is sitting on the corner of my desk, his expression telegraphing *yeah … sure.*

"I'm sorry, he's not available right now."

"Could you tell him it's important?"

The voice is hesitant. "Who is calling, please?"

"Tell him it's Billy Cosgrave." A few moments later, I hear Jim's voice.

"Hey, man, where the fuck are you!"

"Jim! I can't believe it, I just saw you on the cover of a magazine!"

"Where are you? Are you okay, man?"

"I'm working in Calgary. But never mind that. Fill me in!"

"We kept wondering where you were, man," he says. "I wanted to call you, but I didn't have a clue where you were. Things have been happening since you left, Billy."

He tells me about their writing, practices, getting gigs, and ending up as the house band at the rock 'n' roll mecca Whisky a Go Go. Ironically, at one point they wound up playing at Gazzarri's, where Mary had danced. Then along came their first huge hit, "Light My Fire." Their first album went to number two, eclipsed only by the Beatles' *Sgt. Pepper's Lonely Hearts Club Band.* A meteoric rise.

I'm thunderstruck. "Jim, this is so great! Amazing. I never heard you even sing a note!"

"I know, man. It turns out I'm a vocalist." I hear his familiar laugh. "So, you're okay, man? What kind of work are you doing?"

"I work with a new company selling travel to Hawaii and Mexico from across Canada. I really enjoy marketing, and it turns out I'm good at it."

"Huh. Is it interesting?"

"It beats selling subscriptions to the *LA Times*."

"Oh yeah," he laughs, "that gig."

We're both quiet for a beat.

"I can't believe we've connected, man."

"You'll get a kick out of this. The company's called Fun Seekers."

"Seriously, man?"

"Everybody's looking for fun, right?"

"Hey, man, speaking of travel, we're talking about a European tour. Look, give me your number so I can call you back."

I give him my office number, where I'm working long hours.

"Billy, I know this sounds weird, but we're in the middle of recording. I'll call you tomorrow, man."

"Before you go, Jim … how's Mary?"

"Still beautiful. She moved out to Venice not long after you left LA. She rented an apartment above a studio."

"No kidding. Near you and Ray and Dorothy?"

"Not too far. You remember how small Venice is."

"Do you ever see her?"

"Once in a while. I'm seeing a great chick. Wait'll you meet Pam."

"I called Mary's phone, but it said 'no longer in service.'"

"She has an unlisted number. People are bugging her for interviews. You know, because we were together. And you remember how she always guards her privacy."

"I can't wait to see her again."

"Fuck, man, wait'll I tell her we talked. We were worried. Like, 'Where the hell is Billy, man? Is he okay?'"

"Okay, Jim. Talk to you tomorrow."

"Got to go, man. Great to hear your voice. Talk to you tomorrow."

I hang up the phone and look over at John, who is staring at me with his mouth hanging open.

———

The next day: "Hey, man, it's Jim. I was thinking, since you know travel, why don't you come and work with us?" he says.

"What would I do?"

"You can be our travel manager. Like, make all the travel arrangements for our European tour."

I'm speechless.

"You know, flights, hotels, limos — all that."

"Geez, that sounds amazing, Jim."

He has to go again and asks me to call him on Saturday afternoon.

I think about his offer, about this amazing opportunity falling into my lap: a hot rock 'n' roll band. A great friend. I imagine being with him again, hanging out, travelling, the excitement, the craziness, the fun. I could rent my own apartment in LA, stay with Jim until I found a place. And finally see Mary again! Should I go? Hell yes!

But then I remember how often we were stoned. Think about what it would be like being in the rock 'n' roll lifestyle, with the availability of alcohol and drugs and the inevitable partying with Jim. And I know my reckless inclinations to blindly jump into the deep end. I think about all the temptations served on a silver platter.

Am I actually torn?

But for the first time, I feel stable, and it feels good. And I don't want to leave my girlfriend. Our relationship is easy and caring and we're talking about moving in together. Plus, I love my job and the guys I work with. I relish my life, my independence. I'm hesitating, and decide to ask John, my boss and mentor, for advice.

"Hi, Jim."

"When are you coming down, man? I'll get you a ticket."

"Jim, believe it or not, I'm hesitating."

"Are you fucking crazy, man? Come back to LA. You'd love it. Dope, booze, chicks. You wouldn't believe it, man. These crazy chicks follow me. They jump in my car."

I pause.

"You'd love the job, man — a long way from sleeping on a couch, man, or a roof, or under a pier."

"I know, I know. It sounds crazy, Jim — square and straight and not like me."

"So, what's going on, man? Have you got a girlfriend? Are you in love, man?"

"Yeah, but it's not just her. I got tired of being flat broke. I had to borrow a fucking penny from a beggar in Columbus, Jim."

"No kidding, man, a penny?"

"It made me realize I needed a big change in my life."

There is a long pause.

"Are you there, Jim?"

"Yeah, man, I'm just listening and thinking."

"I've finally got some roots and independence. I have an amazing opportunity here."

"Well, you'll have roots and independence back in LA, man. And an amazing opportunity. Money's not a problem."

I'd wrestled with the temptation, actually deciding to quit, thinking that I'd be crazy to turn down this once-in-a-lifetime opportunity. But a long talk with John had convinced me that the wise thing to do was to focus on my career. *Wisdom*, there's a new concept for me. He offered me a promotion. But the icing on the cake was shares in Fun Seekers. Me, a shareholder!

"Man, I get where you're coming from … I guess."

"I want to give this a shot, Jim. I finally have a salary, my own apartment, my own car, and a girlfriend you'd really like."

"Are you sure, man?"

"Actually, no, but I'm going to give this a shot."

"Your call, Billy."

"Either way, now that we've connected, we'll get together soon. I'll fly to LA to see you, and Mary, or you could come here…. Hey, Jim. Can I have your autograph?"

He laughs. "You have to come to LA to get it."

Although he sounds exactly the same, and it feels like no time has passed once we started talking, my head is spinning trying to reconcile Jim the homeless, aimless poet in Venice with Jim the rock star with the number-one hits. All this in less than two years.

"How cool — a famous international rock star."

"Get down here, man. You'd love the whole scene."

"I will for sure, Jim. I just want to see where this job takes me."

"Whatever you want, Billy."

"I always figured that you and Mary would end up back together. It seemed like you two were meant to be."

"I know, man, but when she broke up with me, well, you know. We'd see each other in Venice, but she didn't like what I was doing."

"What were you doing?"

"The same as when you were here. You know, the unemployed, stoned beach life."

"Great times though."

"She wanted me to get a master's degree to 'reach my intellectual potential.'" He laughs. "Instead, I ended up working in a cheesy LA club playing to a handful of customers. She didn't like our music or the booze and drugs." There's a long pause. "She said she didn't think our love would ever die." Another pause. "I wonder."

21: the ascension

The Doors quickly become America's premier rock band, and they explode onto the international scene. Their unique, hard rock/acid rock/blues/jazz sound is combined with provocative lyrics filled with compelling, clever imagery, urging listeners to expand their consciousness, to take a psychedelic journey, to break on through to the other side.

They're on fire. Their creativity explodes. They release seven major hit albums in a row, starting with their first mega album *The Doors*. All seven go gold. The first time a band has had that many consecutive gold records. The band is counterculture, anti-establishment. Their messages are embraced by an audience captivated by their unique sound and spellbound by their front man: Jim, morphing into a sex-jammed rock star on the international stage. He's been dubbed "America's Mick Jagger."

He is getting endless press for his performances and increasingly bizarre booze- and acid-fuelled antics. There are stories emerging about his erratic behaviour: Not showing up for recording sessions. Being late for concerts. Disappearing. I've called Elektra a few times and left messages, including my home number, but I don't hear back until ...

"Hey, man, everything's been crazy and busy. I called the home number you left but no answer. I've been on the road and all that. Sorry we haven't connected sooner, man." His soft voice with the slow Southern drawl. "We're going to headline a show in Toronto in September, man."

"Perfect! We have an office in Toronto. Where are you playing, and what date?"

"Um, hold on...." I hear a muffled voice on the other end. He comes back on the line. "A place called Varsity Stadium, September thirteenth."

"Right on. I'll arrange a business trip to our Toronto office that week."

"We can finally get together, man. I'll arrange passes for you under your name. We can meet at my hotel after the concert."

"What hotel are you booked into?"

"Um, hold on again for a minute."

Back on the line. "It's called the Windsor Arms. Come there after our show. We're on right after John Lennon and Eric Clapton."

I'd been to the hotel before. An upscale boutique place, it definitely didn't scream rock 'n' roll.

"But how're you doing, Billy? Everything good, man? So much to talk about. It'll be great to see you again. See you in Toronto, man!"

Whoa! What a moment this will be.

———

Varsity Stadium, Toronto, a sold-out show with more than twenty thousand in attendance. I see Jim for the first time since we hugged goodbye at the Greyhound station in LA. I had seen the Beatles when they played Maple Leaf Gardens in Toronto. It was complete pandemonium; the screaming so loud that you couldn't hear the band, thousands of cameras flashing in a blinding, continuous light show until they left the stage. This crowd is different. The adoration is palpable, but there is less hysteria, and they're not shrieking.

I'm fascinated as my previously painfully shy friend dominates the stage with primeval screams, leaping, collapsing, dancing, singing. I'm astonished at his metamorphosis. Absolutely astonished! Shy Jim has morphed into an electrifying, mesmerizing performer. I'm speechless. I'm near the front, but he can't see me in this mayhem. I see Ray on the keys. Same cool dude. But there is a blank, vacant look in Jim's eyes. Like they're looking but not seeing. He looks totally wasted.

The Windsor Arms is only a two-minute drive from the stadium. I assume that the Doors have been driven there immediately after they leave the stage, but it takes me over half an hour because of the huge crowd exiting the stadium. I eventually arrive at the elegant hotel, stroll into the lobby, find the house phone, and ask the operator to connect me to his room.

"Hey, Jim, it's Billy, I'm in the lobby. Great show!"

"Hey … man, ah … come on … ah, up." There are long gaps between words. Like his mind is paralyzed, struggling to form even a word. "Where … ah, where are you?"

"I'm here, Jim, right here in the lobby!"

A long pause. "Um, sorry, man. What, ah, what's happening?" He's mumbling. Completely wasted. "So, ah, where ah, are you again, man?"

"Jim, I'm in the lobby, in your hotel," I say. "What's your room number?"

Silence.

"Are you okay, Jim?"

I hear the phone drop. Half a minute passes. Then I hear a rustle. He's back on the line.

"Hey, Jim, is Mary still in Venice? Is she okay?"

"I, um, don't know, man. She was, ah, you know, into, ah spirituality. She left LA, man … I ah, don't know, where … she is."

"Really, Jim? Do you have any idea where I can find her?"

"Try, ah, India, man."

"Jim? Jim? Jim, are you there?"

Nothing.

"Jim? Can you hear me?"

I can hear that the line isn't dead. But there's just background noise. I have an image of him slumped in a chair, the phone in his lap, chin on his chest ... passed out.

"Jim?"

Sitting in the plush lobby chair, I reluctantly place the house phone back on its cradle.

What the hell? Shocked and shattered, my instinct is to go to his room. But can he even answer the door? Do I want to see him incoherent, unable to speak, passed out? What would be the point?

I can't believe this. We had smoked lots of weed, dropped some acid, had some drinks, but he never, ever got to this state. The one time I saw him really drunk was the weekend of our moonlight swim. The person on the other end of the phone was not Jim. I had anticipated the door opening, his shy smile. "Look at you, man."

And me, "But look at you!"

Mary was afraid his excess would "take him deeper into the dark side." Ray, who co-founded the Doors with Jim, and who cared so deeply for him, would refer to this entirely different drunk person as "Jimbo."

I pad across the plush Persian carpet in the empty lobby, nod at the bored clerk behind the front desk, and step out onto St. Thomas Street. Disconsolate, I head down the vacant street to my car. Now wearing a parking ticket on the windshield.

I call the Windsor Arms the next day, but Jim isn't registered. I ask for Ray's room, thinking Jim might be there. But Ray had also checked out.

I board my plane for Calgary the next day feeling distraught and utterly hurt. Looking down at the forever flat prairies, heading for the Rockies, I'm expressionless, wrapped in my utter disappointment. Disillusioned and devastated that our reunion was sabotaged by booze and drugs.

Reportedly, the lyrics of the first three albums were almost all written by Jim, and Ray instinctively knew they were extraordinary; all those poems and thoughts in his notebooks now seeing the light of day. Those words, seen by so few as he filled the pages on the beach, or on the roof, became monster hit songs. And the brilliant, penniless bard on the beach was catapulted into the international spotlight.

During the time we spent together, I never heard Jim talk about any work, other than a college job in the library and his hope to make films one day. But his first job after university would be partnering with Ray to form the Doors, who would end up with seven gold records and dozens of gold and platinum singles.

Their music continues to be popular around the world. They have sold over one hundred million records and remain one of the best-selling bands of all time, selling over one million a year. The greatly anticipated fiftieth anniversary double album, released on September 14, 2019, demonstrated yet again their global popularity.

Jim never seemed remotely interested in material goods. I only ever saw him in jeans or cutoffs and a shirt. He never talked about getting rich. He didn't talk about fame, other than hoping to be known as a poet or perhaps a filmmaker. And I suspect that he disliked the idolatry, which I think he would regard as mindless worship. He loved writing and creating. How many mega stars walk away from it all? In his too-short career, Jim did it twice. The first time after their fourth gold album when he told the band he was leaving to write — but came back to record three more gold albums. The second time was when he told the band that he was moving to an apartment he and Pam had rented in Paris.

22: losing jim

There's a tap on my office door. John, now my business partner, edges in hesitantly. I'm on the phone, but I motion him in. I look at the uncharacteristically grave expression on his face, his serious eyes. "Just a sec, Terry."

"I've just heard some terrible news on the radio, Billy."

My pulse quickens.

"Jim's dead."

I feel the blood drain from my head.

"Are you okay? Your face is grey."

"Where is he? How do you know for certain? How did he die?"

"Apparently, he died in Paris. Lots of rumours, but they think heart attack."

My mind tries to digest this, but it won't register. "Jim died of a heart attack? That's impossible. He's only twenty-seven!" I feel numb, staring blankly at the happy, tropical Fun Seeker posters on my office wall, remembering his surprise when I told him the name of our company.

"Come on, Billy, let's get out of here. We're going for a drink."

We get in his car and turn on the radio. A Doors song comes on. Jim's voice. Then another. The station announcing a switch in programming. They're doing a tribute to Jim.

Back at John's apartment, he turns on the television. The announcer confirms the news from Paris. The station is mining their library to show pictures of Jim.

I'm riding an emotional rollercoaster. Denying it one moment, dreading it the next.

John pours me another drink. Puts his hand on my shoulder. "I'm really sorry, pal."

His caring touch and helpless words move me to tears. The poor guy, not knowing what to do, goes to the other room and comes back, awkwardly handing me a Kleenex. This tender act triggers more silent tears.

The TV station announces that they will be airing a special on Jim and the Doors. My kind friend John coaxes the reminiscences from me: "Tell me again how you two met.... Remind me of the very first time you had a joint with him." He actually gets me laughing through my tears. I sleep in his guest room and wake up with a terrific hangover. John has the news on, a parade of headlines:

JIM MORRISON FOUND DEAD.
DOORS SINGER DEAD IN PARIS.
MORRISON DIES IN PARIS.
INTERNATIONAL ROCK STAR JIM
MORRISON FOUND DEAD IN PARIS
APARTMENT.
JIM MORRISON DEAD AT 27.

The announcement ricochets around the world. Newspapers, televisions, and radios blare out the shocking news. They report that Jim died in Paris on July 3, 1971, but that the news wasn't released until two days later. Less than two years after our aborted get-together in Toronto....

Jim is dead?

For a brief period, there is respite from the grief. The media are reporting a giant hoax. That Jim faked his death. *As if he's actually dead. As if.* But then the French coroner confirms his death and the cause ... heart attack. I feel so terribly sad and so terribly sorry for Jim. The details leak out, and the rumours start. Bereft fans are in denial. There are claims of conspiracy, wild speculation, the wishful "Mr. Mojo Risin'" theory....

This unique, gifted, incredible young man ... gone? He had so much left to do ... and say. I think about the happy, carefree times with Mary and Jim, those penniless halcyon days in Venice. Then his meteoric rise to fame with the Doors as he became an international rock and sex icon, one of the most influential in the history of rock (and so he remains).

Jim was on the cover of *Rolling Stone* magazine nine times, including an issue published ten years after Paris. The headline: *HE'S HOT, HE'S SEXY, AND HE'S DEAD.*

The Village Voice proclaimed him "The first American male sex symbol since James Dean." In just a few years, his behaviour became evermore unpredictable and notorious. He tells an audience: "I don't know about you, but I intend to have my kicks before the whole shit house explodes." His self-destructive drinking became legendary.

His grave in Père Lachaise Cemetery is one of the top tourist attractions in Paris, and recently moved a notch higher since the tragic fire at Notre Dame. His headstone reads, translated from Greek, "True to his own spirit." Jim, it seems, is immortal. His death forever mourned.

Eight years later, another series of shocking headlines would rock the world:

JOHN LENNON SHOT DEAD.

23: finding mary

How did Mary survive the terrible news of Jim's sudden death? I knew that she would be shocked and inconsolable. They had been a magical, brilliant, gorgeous couple. After Jim's death, I tried to find her yet again, but to no avail.

I'd called telephone information off and on over the years, and there was still no phone listing for her. She seemed to have vanished. What had happened to her? Has she changed? Is she still the exquisite woman I cared for so deeply? Who I secretly loved? Is she even alive?

I never forgot her and continued to wonder about her through the years: through girlfriends, world travel, a successful career, a fabulous wife, and two amazing daughters.

Where could she be? An ashram in India? The Himalayas? Peru? I searched without success. I tried to locate her family. Gave up, and searched again. All to no avail. And then, one day, incredibly … I found her.

―――――――

Los Angeles, 2008

I'm back in LA for the first time since leaving Mary and Jim. I'm in town to attend my daughter's engagement dinner at a private member's beach club on Santa Monica Bay, giving a thank-you speech to the host couple in a room full of men and women in cashmere and silk.

Through the ceiling-to-floor oceanview windows I glance to the left and see Santa Monica Pier in the distance — the pier so central to those heady days. As I am addressing these very nice and privileged people, I flash back to crawling under the pier with Jim to roll a joint … and to sleep sometimes.

I'm also wondering about Mary, when it hits me. Of course! Her middle name was Frances. Her stage name was Mary Frances. I'll bet she kept it to protect her privacy and avoid the media when Jim became famous.

I provide that name to a search firm, which comes back with several profiles, and incredibly one that might conceivably be her. Not in some isolated spiritual mecca in a remote corner of the world, but in Hollywood. Have I found the needle in the haystack? There's no phone number, but at least an address.

I expect the GPS to guide me to a sweeping estate in Beverly Hills. I imagine passing through ornate gates along a winding driveway, the scent of jasmine in the soft air. I automatically assume that she had married and would be an elegant grandmother now who has retained her striking beauty. I'm picturing radiant young grandchildren with shiny chestnut-brown hair frolicking on a sweeping emerald lawn, Mary smiling at them from a table on the terrace.

"Continue on I-405. North to Lankershim Boulevard. Take exit 152. Turn left onto Lankershim Boulevard."

What? This doesn't make sense. I'm driving into an area the polar opposite of what I am expecting. Marginal coffee shops and neighbourhood restaurants. A boarded-up store. Listless pedestrians shuffling slowly in the blistering heat.

Now the odd pickup truck. More and more Latinos.

"Continue along Lankershim Boulevard."

This is a mistake. Either the GPS is wrong or it's the wrong Mary.

I enter a semi-industrial area with car repair shops, storage containers surrounded by industrial fencing, used furniture stores. This is a wild goose chase. As if I'd ever find her.

It's hot as hell. No relief from a cloudless sky; sand and dust swirling.

"You will arrive at your destination, 8250 Lankershim Boulevard, in five hundred yards."

I pull into a gravel driveway under a bleached, faded sign: THE VALLEY VILLAGE TRAILER PARK. Someone named Mary Frances may live here, but it sure as hell isn't Mary Werbelow.

A rusty MANAGER sign is nailed onto the weathered door. I knock.

Jesus, this heat. I'm sweating.

There's no answer, so I peer in the dirty windows through torn curtains. Lifeless. Deserted. Brown grass, dying palm trees, withered cactus plants. Everything is dying of thirst, including me. I insert coins into a dented pop machine. Nothing works, including the coin return. No wonder it's dented.

As I walk to the entrance gate a battered car pulls up. The driver punches in numbers and the gate clanks open. Next a pickup truck crunches up to the gate, three Mexican men riding in the back, coming home from work. This is followed by yet another pickup with at least half a million miles on it. The Mexican driver, bronze skin, white shirt, nods at me standing there.

I smile at him. *"Buenos dias, señor."*

He looks surprised. Gives me a gap-toothed grin. *"Buenos dias!"*

I explain in broken Spanish that I am from Canada, that I am trying to find a lost friend. Would he mind if I follow him in when he opens the gate.

"Si, no problema, señor."

"Gracias." My car follows the pickup's cloud of dust. Faded trailers. Yellow grass. Weeds in cracked concrete pads. The place is neglected, run down. A chain-link fence protects a drained swimming pool, its blue vinyl lining bleached and cracked by the remorseless sun. One bent, corroded chaise lounge has toppled on its side. Yellowed newspapers are trapped against the fence. A sign: DANGER, DO NOT ENTER.

Trailers situated randomly on streets form a grid. The place is eerily quiet. I park near a trailer with a TV commercial shrieking through a black iron-barred screen door. I'm about to knock when I leap back in horror. A snarling black pit bull lunges full force at the screen, saliva-soaked fangs snapping. Enraged, it charges again. Suddenly, an enormous woman in a tent-sized muumuu appears, her short blond hair like wet straw. She kicks the dog, "Whaddya want?!"

I ask about Mary.

"I don't know nuthin!" she yells and slams the door in my face.

What the hell am I doing here?

I see smoke behind a trailer. The air is so hot and still that the smoke is rising undisturbed, straight up. In the back is a wide clearing with a barbecue in the middle. Men are standing around drinking beer, smoking. Staring at me. *Where are the women?*

"*Buenos dias, señores. Hablas inglés?*"

"I do, *señor*. How can we help you?"

I explain that I'm from Canada, looking for a woman named Mary.

"There is a strange woman, she lives alone, who we don't see hardly ever. Mostly in the middle of the night watering her flowers."

He speaks in Spanish to one of his friends. "*Si, si, Maria.*"

"We think her name is Mary. Would you like a *cerveza, señor*? It is my birthday."

"*Si, por que no? Gracias.*" (Yes, why not? Thank you!)

I toast him with the cold Corona, "*Salud,*" and wish him happy birthday.

"Can you tell me more about this mysterious Mary, *señor*?"

He pats my shoulder. "Follow me, *señor*." He walks me half a block to a tidy, faded brown trailer half covered by bushes and vines. Some pots with flowers, a bush with red petals by the screen door. Mary loved flowers. A rusted grey compact car is parked beside it.

"Good luck, *amigo*. I hope it is the Mary you are looking for."

Good Lord. Please no.

I knock on the door. Knock again, louder. "Hello, is anyone home? Hello, Mary? Is this Mary Werbelow? It's Billy Cosgrave from Canada. Hello?"

I flash back to my bubbling excitement when I knocked on her door forty-three years ago, waiting breathlessly. I sensed someone on the other side that day. Finally, the apartment door swung open and there she was — breathtaking, radiant, beautiful.

Now all I have is bubbling anxiety. And an envelope to leave if there's no answer.

Dear Mary,

I have been trying to find you for forty-three years. It's Billy Cosgrave. How incredible if this is actually you! When we hugged goodbye, I promised I would repay the ten dollars you gave me. It took a long time, but here it is attached to this note.

If you're not home, please call me @ 310 449 4100. This is my daughter's cellphone. Can you believe that I have a daughter living in LA!

I cannot wait to see you again! Hoping this is you. Could it be?!

xo

Billy

I am pounding on the door of a complete stranger in a dilapidated trailer park. Christ, if it is Mary, how did she end up like this? "Hello! Hello. Is anyone home?" Repeated knocking, but no response. I lean against the trailer wall. Waiting ... for what? I look around. It's desolate. Two young guys slouch past, averting their eyes. I knock again, call out her name.

Jesus, Bill, get out of here.

I ease down onto the doorstep.

I sit for twenty more minutes. Not sure why. Or what I'm waiting for. What a soulless place. It's time to go. Opening the screen door, I take the letter from my back pocket and get down on my knees to slide the envelope through the mail slot in the door. Lifting the cover, I peek inside.

Jesus Christ! My heart slams into my ribs. I freeze. A pair of legs in grey sweatpants is standing dead still an inch from the door. I bolt up, envelope now shaking in my hand.

How long has that person been standing there?

Talking to the door, I say, "Is your name Mary? It's Billy from Canada."

A painfully long pause follows. There's no response. The silence is eerie. I know someone is standing three inches from me.

Then a thin, hesitant voice. "Billy? Billy Cosgrave?"

"Yes. Is that you, Mary?"

The heat is stifling. Is she still there?

Click. A key sliding into a lock. Then more excruciating silence. Did she just lock the door? Christ, the tension! A glint of sun catches my eye as the metal handle starts to turn. The door cracks open. I see strands of wispy grey hair. The door is opening imperceptibly. I catch a glimpse of pallid skin. Then a face.

My heart sinks. A hauntingly thin woman, her bony shoulders protrude through a faded grey sweatshirt, matching grey sweatpants barely clinging to nonexistent hips. Long, straight, uncombed grey hair. Zero makeup. Intelligent brown eyes, Bardot lips.

My God, it's her.

She's looking at me, dazed. "How did you find me?"

She opens the screen door and steps outside. Cautious. Dishevelled. Staring at me. "I usually sleep all day. I'm ill and on meds. The drugs make me drowsy." Speaking slowly. Glancing around suspiciously. She is obviously sick, trying to focus.

I'm trying to be calm and not betray my shock at seeing her. My search is finally over, but it is the ghost of Mary that I've found.

"I've been trying to find you since I left LA, Mary. It's taken me so long. I almost gave up trying to find you." She's studying me. "I found Jim after I saw him on the cover of a magazine. I couldn't believe it!"

Mary, in her reedy, thin voice, a hint of a smile. "You're not the only one."

"He said you were fine, and had moved to Venice, but couldn't remember your unlisted number. Then the last time we talked he said you had gone to India."

She is nodding. "He got a hold of me to tell me you guys had connected. What a relief to know you were okay. We had no idea where you were for, what, almost two years?" She looks off into the distance. "We were worried about you." A weak smile. "Can you believe he became a famous rock star?"

"We never heard him hum or sing."

Another smile. "Not only that, but he couldn't dance either. Can you believe it?" The fog is lifting. "I remember he said he offered you a job. Something to do with travel, wasn't it?"

I nodded.

My emotions are ricocheting from heartbreak to nervous excitement, from huge relief that she is alive to profound sorrow for her situation.

"I broke Jim's heart, Billy, and his death broke mine. He thought we would get back together, and I promised we would, but ..." She looks wistful. "He just went farther and farther into booze and drugs. Into the dark side. I'm sure you knew about his girlfriend, Pam. He met her when the Doors were unknown, playing in a cheesy club."

"I only read about her and saw pictures of her and Jim together."

"Well, I met her in Venice. She was the worst thing that ever happened to him. She was doing drugs. Heroin, cocaine. Exactly what Jim didn't need — an enabler."

She has a look of resignation in her eyes. "She was with him in

Paris when he died. The coroner said he was dead in the bathtub and that the cause of death was a heart attack. What twenty-
seven-year-old has a natural heart attack? I believe the theory that
he found some of her heroin after coming home drunk and over-
dosed." She sighs. "If he wasn't living with a heroin addict, he
might be alive today."

We are both silent.

"It's been forty-three years since you and Jim dropped me off at
the Greyhound station, Mary." I smile at her.

She perks up, and I hear a hint of her lilting laugh. "How could
I forget those blue eyes!"

"Where do we begin, Mary?"

She is so frail and unsteady, but is becoming more alert. Her
spirits are lifting. It's like she's being energized before my eyes. I'm
seeing some traces of the Mary I once knew emerge, the familiar
current of excitement that would amplify her conversation.

As the memories surface, she becomes animated, her remarkable recall filling in the blanks. But we've been standing for ages.
I'm hoping she'll invite me in.

Instead, she sits on the step and makes room for me. "Sit
down, Billy."

"Remember how I hated drinking? Well, he'd come back after
some crazy event and show up at my place. Always sober. I had an
apartment above a studio in Venice. We'd talk and talk. We never
stopped loving each other, but it was impossible as he got wilder,
drunker, and drugged." She looks wistful again. "Nothing was going to get in the way of his pursuit of the dark side."

"The last time I talked to him was in his Toronto hotel after a concert. He was so drunk he was incapacitated. He passed out on the phone."

She nods. "That's what I mean. He was so sweet, but the hard drinking brought out his demons ... or created them."

"I went to the concert," I say. "It was the first time I'd seen him since LA. His performance left me speechless. He had told me from LA to come to his room at the hotel in Toronto. He was completely out of it, Mary. I was shattered. It was going to be our big reunion."

"I never went to a concert," she says. "I heard they played to huge audiences and that Jim was riveting and controversial. Also chaotic." She paused, sighing. "He was fascinated with chaos and the unpredictable."

"I was absolutely stunned," I tell her. "That transformation from gentle and shy Jim to this mesmerizing personality on stage. And what a voice!"

Conversation flows. Her eyes are coming to life, her voice enthusiastic. So many memories flooding back. "I can't believe it's you! Remember when you'd come and see me at the nightclub? Dancing like crazy? All that energy? All those people? What fun all that was!

"Remember when you crashed the Academy Awards?" She's laughing and clapping her hands. "The great times that we had!"

I'm hiding my despair at the situation she's in — her health, her appearance, her trailer. But she is coming back.

"You know, Jim would send me poems, letters, things like that, before and after we broke up. I have all these things from him. Nobody knew the gentle, sweet Jim.

"Are you married, Billy? Do you have a family?"

I tell her about my wife and two daughters.

"Hilary, my eldest, just got engaged and recently moved to LA with her fiancé. That's why I'm here. For her engagement dinner and to meet the in-laws."

"Are you kidding? You have a daughter living in LA? How ironic! And you never came back to LA after we dropped you at the Greyhound station?"

"No, I didn't."

"I never thought I'd see you again. And here you are! Unbelievable, Billy!"

"How about you, Mary. Do you have a family?"

"I had two children … and divorced them both."

I look confused.

"I was married twice."

I burst out laughing.

The years melt away as we reconnect. She seems tired but energized, zigzagging from one topic to the next. Her eyes look brighter and happier.

"How long have you been living here, Mary?"

She looks around. "You mean living like this? Too long. Nothing I did in this life would cause me to be in this current situation. I'm not a victim. This is from a past lifetime."

"Before Jim passed out, I asked him where you were, and he said 'Try India.'"

Mary's expression is pensive. "The only place I felt at home was India. It's the first time that my soul felt comfortable." She stares off into space, then seems to snap back. "Oliver Stone offered me money when he was making his film on the Doors. I refused because I knew he wouldn't portray the shy, kind, loving Jim that you and I knew. You never heard Jim say a bad thing about anyone, and he wasn't judgmental. But I knew that Stone would make it all one-sided, sensationalize the excess and make him look bad. Showing Jim at his worst. He offered me more money, but I still refused. And I was right: he screwed it up just how I knew he would."

"I read that Ray was outraged at the film and its portrayal of Jim. He despised Oliver Stone," I say.

"I liked Ray. I didn't particularly like the music, but he seemed very centred and mature. He was a cool person in a good way," she replied.

Looking at her situation, I'm reminded of her stubborn integrity. Refusing money on principle — in spite of her dire circumstances.

We've been talking for a very long time. Her mind is starting to wander. "I need to sleep," she says. "I'm tired all the time, and sick."

"Do you know what causes this, Mary?"

"I've been diagnosed with MCS."

"What is that?"

"Multiple Chemical Sensitivity. When I lived in Venice the place below me used chemicals, which I got exposed to. I have negative reactions to so many toxic things. Cigarette smoke is terrible. Car exhaust. The air is full of pollutants. I water my plants at three in the morning because the air is a little better."

She seems utterly alone. She looks at me. Lonesome Mary.

"You know, I was praying for a miracle before I went to sleep, and woke up to you knocking on the door."

"I never forgot you. I loved you, Mary, very much."

She gives me a meek, gentle smile. "I know you did Billy. I have to lie down. I'll get you my phone number and you can call me."

She comes back outside with her number written on a piece of paper. We hug goodbye. I can smell her stale breath.

I leave with an aching sadness, full of grief for her situation.

I call her the next day and we talk for over an hour, until I can hear her fading.

"I need to sleep, Billy. I'm weak. I can't talk any longer."

"No problem, Mary, I'll call you tomorrow."

"Hi, Mary, it's a beautiful day. Let's go for lunch at a nice restaurant on the ocean."

Her mood has switched. "I told you I'm ill. I can't go out at all. It's the MCS."

I'm startled by her tone. She was so engaging and enthusiastic on the phone yesterday.

"Everything in the air would make me sicker if we went to a restaurant. The pollution in the air, the car exhausts, the smell of perfume. Don't you understand that?"

"Well, won't the Pacific breeze be clean and refreshing? Won't it be good for you?"

"People will be wearing perfume and other toxic scents."

"Even perfume makes you sick?"

"Of course it does — it's all chemicals. Please don't wear aftershave or deodorant when you come here."

"No problem. Mary, I want to help you. So what can I do for you?"

"If you ask a question … you know the answer."

Pardon?

"Good intentions pave the way to Hell."

I'm trying to digest this.

"Speech at its best is an honest lie."

"I'm not following you, Mary."

"Every religion has a candle. The flickering is like the mind. The flickering must be still, as the mind must be still to find enlightenment. Do you understand, Billy? I know that I know — it is beyond mind, beyond knowing, beyond intellect."

She can't see the bewildered expression I'm wearing.

"They're trying to evict me. There was a lawyer on my roof last night."

"I'm coming out there tomorrow, Mary."

"No, I don't want to see anybody. I'm too sick."

"But you need help."

"No one gets out of here in one lifetime, Billy."

"I'll be there around noon tomorrow."

———

The next day she's so groggy and spacey. Is it the drugs? Is her mind going?

"Mary, obviously you need help."

"Did you know that Jim wrote 'The End' about me? He told me that many of the songs in the albums were about me. 'The End,'

'Love Her Madly,' 'Moonlight Drive,' 'The Crystal Ship,' a bunch more." She starts reciting the lyrics for "The Crystal Ship."

"I didn't know that, Mary. All those famous songs! I honestly thought you two would be together forever," I say. "I was so stunned when you broke up."

"He needed to learn about life. And so did I. He never wanted to be a rock star, you know. He just wanted to be a poet and writer." There's a long silence, then she starts quoting more lines from Jim's poetry. Then more silence. "Last night I was remembering all our times together in LA, Billy. So few people knew the sweet, gentle, loving Jim. I decided that I want to give you the private tapes, poems, all of it. You and Jim were close. I know how you cared for him. You should have them." A far off look comes into her eyes. "I've been saving them for so long."

Illness has taken its toll. Her flowing, shiny chestnut-brown mane is now wispy and grey.

"I'm really very sick, Billy. I fell and hit my head, and since then my mind goes all over the place. I imagine things."

"Mary, let me take you to a hospital right now."

"I'll NEVER go back to a hospital! They'll kill me with their toxic drugs and poison me with their chemical-laced food."

"Well, what do you want to do? You need medical attention."

"I'll take care of myself."

There's that fierce independence.

She switches subjects. "Remember how broke you two were? And you got that weird job with that guy in the red Rolls-Royce?"

We chuckle at that.

"How simple life was then, Billy." She is very diminished, and I am worried.

"Mary, I have to fly back to Canada. What are we going to do about your situation if you won't let me take you to a hospital? Can I call a doctor?"

"No."

"Well, here's my phone number. Please call me anytime, night or day. Here's my email address, too."

"I don't use email."

"Well, then, please call me. And I'll be calling you."

In a tight farewell hug, she feels so fragile. Like a tiny bird. My eyes are glistening.

Walking to my car, I turn, and we exchange a smile. She waves weakly. My God, how did this happen? From a blazing comet to a barely flickering candle. Christ, this stunning sorrow.

I wonder if I'll ever see her again. I barely get to my car before my eyes fill with tears.

24: this is the end

Nine months later, I'm back in LA.

"The number you have dialed is not in service...."

Here we go again. *Jesus, I hope she's okay.* Maybe I misdialed. I punch in the numbers again. *Come on, Mary, come on, answer your phone!* The detached voice: "The number you have dialed ..."

Damn! She hasn't replied to my letters. I implored her to call, to let me know if she needs help. Her health is failing — stealing more of her.

"I'm not connected to the web; I don't get email. You'll have to call me."

But her phone is disconnected.

Mysterious, enigmatic Mary.

———

Sunday morning, North Hollywood.

Where is everybody? It's abnormally quiet. Has Hollywood been evacuated? What gives?

Parking in an almost vacant parking lot, I wander into a mahogany-panelled café. "A cappuccino, please," I tell a cheerful barista. I receive a disinterested, flickering glance from a couple, eyes snapping back to their iPhones. There's only one other patron. A guy with long hair, prominent cheekbones, taut, pale skin, day-old beard. He's staring intently at his laptop screen. Focused. He snaps his thumb. An inspiration! He continues tapping out his masterpiece.

Back in the car, I'm anxious and increasingly worried about my next stop — The Valley Village Trailer Park.

I pull into the gravel driveway. Stones pop under the tires, gravel crunches as the wheels grind to a halt, dust-coated brakes squealing. There's no shade from the dead palm fronds. A sudden hot draft swirls upward, a miniature tornado swirling the dust and sand.

CRACK. Christ! A gunshot?

A giant brown palm branch crashes down. My heart is pounding.

The gates are locked. The dry air is stifling. A pickup on its last legs, front bumper missing, pulls up in front of the gates.

I approach the driver, who has dark, weathered skin. *"Buenos dias, señor."*

He looks at me. I explain that I am from Canada and visiting *mi amiga*, my girlfriend. Can I come in with him? He gives me a gold-toothed grin. *"No problema, señor."* He leans over and forces open the dented passenger door.

The place looks worse than ever. Like an abandoned cemetery. Only a handful of trailers are left, surrounded by cracked concrete pads. I point to unit 9. He stops and lets me out. A thick film of dust blankets Mary's car — windows coated, upholstery cracked, rusted plates expired. The left tire is deflated — the car sits on an angle beside her faded, bleached trailer. The flowers she would water at three in the morning now dead. The lifeless vines slumped onto the parched, cracked earth. I rap at the door.

"Mary … are you there?" Then louder: "Mary? Mary! It's Billy."

I can hardly breathe.

I sense motion out of the corner of my eye — a shrunken, elderly Mexican woman struggling into a white plastic chair by her trailer. I approach her. She is so stooped she can't look me in the eyes. It's almost a hundred degrees — she's dressed in black. *"Buenas dias, señora. Hablas inglés?"*

"No, señor. Solo español."

I learn that she lives here with her son. But she doesn't understand my twisted Spanish. Points to the door and yells, *"Miguel!"*

Rubbing his eyes, Miguel steps into the blistering sun. He speaks English. He's been sleeping before he goes to work. "I work in the night and sleep in the day," he explains.

"I own a food truck, *señor*," he proudly informs me. He has lived with his mother in the trailer park since his father died.

I gesture toward trailer number nine, explaining to Miguel that I am Mary's friend.

"We haven't seen her in many, many weeks, *señor*. The last time I saw her was in my headlights at three in the morning. That's when I return from work ... she was trying to water her flowers."

"Have you seen any lights in her trailer? Like TV light or anything?"

"Nothing, *señor*. But when I last saw her, she had a cane. She was very thin, *señor*."

The widow, matter-of-fact: *"Ha muerto?"* Is she dead?

Miguel looks at me.

Startled, I manage a *"Muchas gracias, Miguel, y señora."*

Filled with dread, I return to Mary's and open the screen door. "Mary! Mary!"

I'm now pounding on the door as the widow watches me from her chair.

There's a terrible silence. Still, stultifying. Everything is baked and brown.

Maybe she's gone away? I walk around the trailer, looking for wires feeding inside. Is the power on? The phone? The water? I pick up the cracked hose — dry and brittle, the connector rusting.

Back to the door. "Mary!"

I get on my knees to pry open the mail slot and peer in, desperately hoping to see her sweatpanted legs standing silently on the other side. "Are you home? Are you in there? Mary, please answer me!"

Once again I have brought a letter in case she doesn't answer. I slide it in and hear it slap on the linoleum floor.

I stand up and sigh, despair turning to dread. Inexplicably, I reach for the door handle, always locked against the forces of the outside world. "They're trying to evict me," she had told me gravely. I twist the handle. It gives. I turn it, inching the blistered door open. *BANG!* My heart stops. Dead silence. What the hell was that? I pause, then ease farther inside. A metal cane, propped against the door, has been dislodged and fallen to the floor.

Gut-wrenching tension as I ease the door open and edge a foot inside. "Mary! Hello! Is anybody here?"

I am in a sea of clutter. Heavy curtains subdue the light. Fabric is draped over bookshelves and stacked boxes, like being inside a boarded-up museum. Dust motes hang suspended in the dead air. "Mary!"

To the right, three stairs lead to an impossibly blocked kitchen. An enormous overstuffed antique chair faces an old television. "Mary?"

At the end of the narrow kitchen a door stands open. The end of a bed is visible in the muted, beige light. Inching closer, the silence is excruciating. "Mary! It's Billy!"

Quieter than a tomb — except for the goddamned clock. My nerves are crackling. Almost at the door, the clock is so fucking loud — *tick, tock, tick, tock.* My forehead is beaded with sweat.

The bedspread is formed into a miniature tepee by a pair of feet. Heart-stopping fear grips me as I ease into the cramped room. My eyes scan up from her feet to thin legs that barely ruffle the surface. Her chest beneath the spread is motionless. Mouth open — eyes closed. There is no sound. In the midst of this heartbreaking moment, I notice that her hair is shorter. "Mary, Mary, it's Billy." Again, "Mary!" Nothing.

Resisting the urge to bolt, I back up slowly. Wide-eyed and trembling, I reach the door, stumbling over her fallen cane.

Outside, gulping in the fresh air, I clutch my phone. Frantically dial 911.

Soon, a high-pitched scream. Then another. Louder and closer. I shout and wave furiously as the giant fire truck thunders into the driveway, an ambulance on its tail. Lights flashing, sirens wailing. The vehicles grind to a halt.

"Number nine!" I yell up to the driver. The fire engine seems two storeys tall. I'm wondering how they'll get past the gate when it magically opens. They cut the sirens. Gravel crunches under the gigantic tires on their way to number nine.

A police car arrives. Emergency vehicles line up at Mary's refuge. I brief them, and in they go. Christ, the anxiety.

How could so many huge, athletic guys fit into such a small space?

The captain emerges, his men gathered round.

"She's alive. But she's very frail and sick and needs to be hospitalized."

"Great," I say, "I'll follow the ambulance."

"We can't take her into the ambulance, since she refused."

"But she's obviously terribly ill. Why can't you?"

"Under California law, if we take someone against their will, it's considered kidnapping."

"Are you serious?"

"Although this woman is marginally coherent, and very weak, we need her permission."

I'm stunned. "So, you leave her here to die?" I can see the impotence in their eyes. "This is insane!"

"If she was unconscious, we could take her to the hospital under the 'implied consent' provision. But she's conscious."

"Who is she?" they ask.

"Mary Werbelow. She's a friend of mine," I say. "And Jim Morrison's ex-girlfriend."

"WHAT!"

So, I tell these *GQ* guys the abridged version. They are transfixed. "No kidding! Wow! Amazing! Unbelievable! Holy shit." They are pumped, then solemn. "Take care, buddy. I wish we could help her."

"By the way, this trailer park is ... strange. We were called here a few months ago to another trailer. The man was over eighty. We looked around and found intimate photos of Ronald Reagan, very personal — in his bedroom, wearing pyjamas, dressing gown, and so on."

I look at them, amazed.

"Apparently, he had been Reagan's personal photographer for years. Again, I'm sorry we can't help your Mary."

They leave me standing outside unit nine. Mary's alive? How can this be? I knock on the door. This time it's locked. I call out her name. No reply. I go to the side, where I now know her bedroom is. The emergency men had opened the small window. "Mary, it's Billy. I want to come in."

A feeble voice: "No, I don't want to see anybody."

"But you need help."

"I don't want any help."

"I will bring you juice, and water, and food, Mary."

"No."

"But you need help," I plead.

Silence. More silence.

"Mary, if you won't let me in, and won't let me help you, I can't do anything. If you say okay, I'll wait until you're ready — as long as you want."

"I don't want to see anybody."

"But if you won't let me in, at some point I'll have to leave. And then what will you do?"

"How did the ambulance get here?"

"I called 911."

"Don't ever do that again."

Silence.

"Mary, this makes no sense."

Silence.

"If you won't let me in, you'll be all alone."

No response.

"Okay then. I'm leaving."

I sit on the dehydrated grass outside her window for half an hour. Dead quiet. Listening. Waiting.

Feeling hopeless and helpless, I knock on the widow's door. Miguel answers. I explain the situation and give him my phone number in Canada.

"Please call me if anything happens, Miguel. Please."

He's kind and sympathetic. "Don't worry, *señor*, I promise to call."

I phone Social Services and explain how critical the situation is. The caseworker says, "I'll make this a priority, and get on it right away."

"I'm from Canada," I tell her. "I don't live here, so I can't check in on her."

"Don't worry. Give me your number. We'll give this priority and go and see her right away," adding gently, "We'll call you if anything happens."

Once again, the kindness of strangers.

This seemingly endless day is finally coming to an end. Emotionally exhausted, I get into my car, turn the key, and ask Siri for directions.

———

The next night at the United check-in counter at LAX. I present my passport and bag and clear security. Sitting in the pre-boarding lounge studying the faces, I notice not very many people are waiting to board. The airline exec part of me muses that with such a low load factor, this flight is losing money. I approach the check-in supervisor and request a frequent flier upgrade.

"You'll be the only one in Business Class." A pleasant smile as she hands me my revised boarding pass.

Cabin lights are dimmed for takeoff. There's a hush as we ascend. From my window seat, the billion watts below illuminate

LA. It looks like a gigantic computer chip. My mind flashes back to Mary on her stage, illuminated by spotlights and strobe lights, a free spirit dancing in her blissful prime. Electric and electrifying. Unrestrained. Joyful, almost ecstatic. On top of the world.

As the plane banks out over the jet-black Pacific, I see the meandering ribbon of Sunset Boulevard, the street lights illuminating Ocean Boulevard, the twinkling shorelines of Venice and Santa Monica Beach.

Soaring away from the glittering coast, the lights fade and disappear. I look down and spot a solitary light flickering on the sea of darkness — a vessel gliding alone into the night.

My reflection in the window is blurred by tears. I hear Jim's song to Mary, his aching lament.

This is the end … beautiful friend.

25: mary has died, señor

"Hello?"

"Is this *señor* Bill?"

"Yes, is this Miguel?"

"*Sí, señor*. I have sad news." His voice is fading in and out. Typical LA cell reception.

"Mary has died, *señor*. I am sorry to tell you this news."

I freeze. It's Miguel, who lives in the trailer within sight of Mary's. I have called this good man to check on Mary since my last visit when I called 911, after she refused to see me, and refused my offer to help. He has ever more disheartening news. He saw her with a cane, he saw her with a walker, he saw her trip and fall.

"When did she die, Miguel?"

"Three weeks ago, *señor*, at the beginning of May. I'm sorry I didn't call you sooner, but I couldn't find your number. My mother found it this morning."

"What happened, Miguel?"

"My neighbour saw a pickup truck pull into her place, remove everything, and drive away. After the truck left, I went and checked and her trailer was completely empty."

"What about her car?"

"A few days later they towed her car away. I never saw her drive it. Then yesterday her trailer was demolished and now there is nothing. I'm sorry to tell you this, *señor* Bill."

I slump in my chair and sigh. I shouldn't be shocked, but I am, and crestfallen. She was so thin and ill the last time I saw her. Enigmatic, mysterious Mary. What a life she led. From centre stage to a total recluse.

One visit, she was fully engaged, eyes sparkling with detailed memories and facts. Next time, she was distracted, gazing off into space, losing her train of thought. She was somewhere else. "There was a lawyer on my roof last night with an eviction notice." Dead serious.

"Thank you for calling me, Miguel."

"You are welcome, *amigo*. If ever you come to Los Angeles, I would enjoy to see you."

"*Muchas gracias*, Miguel. I really appreciate your call."

I'm alone at home.

What the hell? That's it?

I am overcome with sorrow. My lips begin to tremble, warm tears slide down my cheeks. Not bothering to wipe them, I sit in stunned silence feeling numb and disconnected. Not unlike I felt when the media pounced on the news of Jim's sudden death and blasted it around the world. Is there a protocol for reacting to death? Should I be wailing, gnashing my teeth?

My best friend, Gary, who had picked me up in Ohio, shockingly died at age thirty-one. His frantic mother tried to throw herself into the grave with her son when the first shovelful of dirt thudded indifferently onto his mahogany coffin.

As friends and family die, I feel the sorrow seeping in. Intellectually resigned to the fact, but emotionally gasping for breath. Will we ever grasp the concept of permanent absence ... permanent loss? No second chance when it comes to death ... unless you have certain beliefs.

Jim, Mary, and me. Two out of three have left the building. Could I have done more when I finally found her? I visited her, called her, implored her to let me help. I called the ambulance — she sent it away. I called Social Services. She shooed them away. She was fiercely independent right to the end.

I remember her private mementoes of Jim. "I want you to have them, Billy. You knew how we were. You knew the real Jim. The real story." The history of Mary and Jim dumped into a mysterious pickup truck. Consigned then ... to a city dump?

"Miguel, does anyone know where the pickup went? Who drove it? Anything?"

"No, *señor*, we don't know anything."

———

Five months later, I'm back in Los Angeles.

"Hello, Miguel, it's *señor* Bill."

"How are you, *señor*?"

"Fine, thank you, Miguel. I'm back in LA and wondering if you have heard anything more about Mary?"

"No, *señor*. But the manager lady will be here on Monday. Maybe she can help you."

"Thank you, Miguel. I gave up trying to call them a long time ago. They never returned my phone calls. The one time that I got through to enquire about Mary, they hung up on me."

"*Si, señor*, they were terrible, but they are gone. A new owner came. The manager lady, Veronica, she is nice."

———

Siri: "Exit the 405 in one mile, take the I-5 to North Hollywood."

My daughter Whitney is deftly manoeuvring through the clogged arteries that are LA's freeways. I glance at her serene face, marvelling at her confidence as she bullets along. I am not serene as we pull onto the gravel driveway of the now-familiar Valley Village Trailer Park.

On each previous visit I would knock on the manager's door repeatedly, even though there was a seemingly permanent CLOSED sign propped between the dirty window and the stained curtains.

I decide to forgo the pointless ritual and instead walk directly to the locked gate. Peering through the bars, I search for number nine, Mary's place. Her trailer and the dust-coated car with the expired plate have both vanished. As if they had been an illusion. Even though I expected this, I'm aghast. My heart sinks. So that's it? Erased without a trace?

The grounds look much cleaner. The weeds have been whacked. The grass is green. Even the gate has a fresh coat of white paint. There are kids splashing in the pool. Whitney stands by her car, watching me. I half-heartedly approach the office door expecting the usual. Instead, a cheery sign reads WELCOME! and is bordered by miniature hand-painted flowers.

I knock.

A pleasant voice responds. "Come in, please."

The door opens to the bright smile of a pretty Latina woman in her late thirties.

"Hi. Are you Veronica?"

"Yes, I am. How can I help you?"

"And you're the manager?"

"I am."

I introduce myself and my daughter.

She stands to shake our hands. "Are you looking for a rental?"

"No, actually we're here about Mary Werbelow."

"The one and only Mary Werbelow!" Her sincere dark eyes are twinkling.

"Mary was my dear friend. I lived with her when I came to LA in 1965. I visited her here at Valley Village several times."

Veronica is wearing a pleasant smile.

"She called me her Canadian cousin. Were you here when she died?"

"Oh no … I'm so sorry!" The smile vanishes. "I knew she'd been sick a long time. Still, I'm so terribly sorry to hear this. She was such an unusual woman; I really cared for her."

She pauses, distraught. "She was my favourite. Sometimes we would talk for an hour, even longer. She was two different people. She'd be vague and act very strange. Then her eyes would focus and she would tell me stories about her life." She pauses again, reflecting. "Especially about Jim Morrison. Mary had an amazing memory. Her eyes would turn bright and happy talking about their times together. Then she'd become doleful and melancholy. It's so tragic that he died so young. I'm so sad that she has passed."

I look around her office, the sun spilling in on fresh curtains, her pristine desk. There is a picture of a pretty Latina girl in a graduation gown — a younger replica of Veronica, friendship cards on her credenza, a framed quotation about love. Veronica obviously has a big heart.

Her eyes soften, and she gazes out the window. "I remember Mary more than anyone else in the park. She had a fascinating mind and would talk about many things. Sometimes I would hear that she was out in the middle of the night, sitting in a yoga position, other times watering her flowers — at three in the morning. A very unusual woman.

"She would tell me that she was worried that her treasured Jim Morrison mementoes would end up with Mike if something happened to her. She was insistent that she didn't want him to have them."

"Mike?"

"Her long-divorced ex-husband."

So she wasn't completely isolated!

"Mary would get a pensive look in her eyes when she talked about Jim. It sounds like they truly were soulmates. I think she never stopped loving him." Veronica looking quizzical. "It's strange that you arrived today with the news about Mary," she says. "I just got a call this morning from the North Hollywood Police Department. She called them so much that they were on a first-name basis with her. She drove them crazy with her complaints about somebody smoking in the next trailer, too loud music, and so on, but they liked her. They were concerned because her phone calls had stopped. They wondered if she was okay."

"Do you know what happened to her belongings? Anything about the pickup truck that showed up and took them?"

"Oh yes, that was Mike."

Her ex-husband has her possessions?

"So, that would have been in May?"

"Oh no, that was in February." Looking downcast, she asks. "When did she die? This is so sad."

"In May," I reply.

Veronica looks at me, at Whitney, back at me. There is a puzzled look on her face. After a long pause, she hesitantly says, "This is going to sound very strange, but ... are you sure Mary is dead?"

Whitney and I exchange glances.

"Why, yes, I was told by her neighbour Miguel that she died in May and that her trailer was demolished."

"Well, it's true that we demolished her trailer in May, but she had gone."

"Gone?" I can't even blink.

"Yes, she moved out in February after the court sided with us in the eviction dispute. We paid Mary the amount the court determined, and she moved out."

What the hell? My mind is racing. "Do you have any idea what happened to her?"

"No idea whatsoever." She methodically checks all her files. "People leave all the time with no notice, no forwarding address, no information whatsoever. You wouldn't believe what they leave behind! Personal belongings, clothes, even photo albums!"

She searches through her filing cabinet, then her desktop computer. "I'm sorry, but her files have been removed from the cabinet and deleted from the computer. I have nothing."

Thinking, she opens her purse and removes her cellphone. "There's a slim chance I have something in my personal cell." Her thumbs tap away. Then scroll. A look of disappointment comes over her. "Darn, I have nothing here either."

She stares out her window. "She's simply vanished."

We thank Veronica for her time and help. I give her my phone number and implore her to call me if she hears anything at all.

"Of course I will."

She stands and walks us to the door, surprising us each with a hug. "It was nice to meet you. Don't worry, I will contact you if ever I hear anything," she says. Then, "Whitney, why don't you give me your phone number as well."

Flying out of LAX three nights later, the cabin lights lowered, I focus on the familiar coastal lights until they disappear. Staring intently down at the sea, I remember my last flight and the single fading light of a solitary boat heading out into the pitch-black sea.

———

Three weeks later, I am at home, sitting in my silent den. The desk lamp casts a muted glow over the photos that surround me. Mary staring straight into the camera, a slight smile on her lips, lustrous chestnut-brown hair framing her intelligent, lovely face. Her left hand rests on the hip of her white slacks; a beaded necklace around the neck of her wine-coloured sweater. This unique, stunning, enigmatic woman —

I'm jolted from my thoughts by the phone.

"Hello, Bill? This is Veronica from Valley Village Mobile Park."

"Hello! How are you, Veronica?"

"I'm fine, thank you. I hope you're sitting down, Bill. You won't believe this." There's a long pause. "Mary's alive."

Veronica had found a number for Mary's long-divorced ex-husband, Mike. When he told Veronica that Mary was, in fact, alive, she asked if he could please have Mary call her.

"I told him that I really needed to talk to her."

"Veronica, this is unbelievable! If he is able to contact her, and she calls you, please call me. Or ask her to call me. Please!"

But we never hear from Mary. I wonder if she even got the message.

Her home has been demolished and Mary has vanished. With her photographic memory of an extraordinary life and her treasured collection of Jim memorabilia.

26: la honours the doors

I'm in LA for Christmas with my family, driving from Pacific Palisades to Westchester, when I decide to stop in Venice en route. What the hell? Jim's face dominates the front page of the newspaper. It's the cover of the Doors's first smash hit album. The headline: *LOS ANGELES HONORS THE DOORS.*

There will be a dedication ceremony: "The Doors put Venice on the map forever and transformed rock 'n' roll around the world." LA is officially declaring January 4 as the "Day of the Doors."

I move my car to a longer-term parking spot near the Venice Pier to find out where it will be held. I decide to stroll along the beach to

Westminster Avenue — to the building where Jim slept on the roof. I lean against a wall and drink in the breathtaking view of sparkling Santa Monica Bay. I walk along the familiar shoreline from Venice to the Santa Monica Pier. Memories roll in like the waves.

Later, as I am unlocking my car, two couples walk by. "Just think, guys, right here, right here is exactly where Jim Morrison walked!" Pointing at the beach, excited: "And that's the actual beach where he hung out and wrote his songs. I mean … fucking unbelievable! Can you imagine that?"

The following week, I'm sitting on a bench in Venice on a warm afternoon. The heady scent of freshly cut grass, the ubiquitous LA sound of leaf blowers. A classic California day. Sunny, warm, soft. I'm recalling how Jim loved the endless procession of beautiful days, the carefree beach life, the gentle, warm breezes. Living in the moment. When life was intoxicating. When youth were engaged, energized, outraged, demanding change. When a young Jim Morrison screamed, "We want the world, and we want it now!"

I see the irony of where I am, back in Venice. The joyful sound of children yelping and squealing as they stampede across the playground. Too far away to make out their faces, but close enough to hear their laughter. A herd of happy, guileless children in their school uniforms. Their high-pitched, gleeful chattering. Running, skipping.

A beautiful kindergartener cuts from the herd. A handsome young blond boy chases her. They're in a heated race and I'm the finish line. The little girl with her chestnut-brown hair in a bobbing ponytail, tunic swirling. Her first-grade brother, tie undone, white shirt untucked. Bearing down on me with outstretched arms.

"Pappa!"

Their sky-blue eyes are full of bright tomorrows. Holding a tiny hand on either side, I escort them to their mother's black SUV and buckle them in.

"How about an ice cream cone, kids!"

We drive to a landmark ice cream shop in Venice. Perched on three stools right at the window, we're watching the people of Venice passing by.

A particularly striking young couple strolls arm in arm toward us. Carefree. Blissful. Full of life. A gorgeous couple. I imagine them stopping, then peering in the window. Our eyes lock. The long-haired guy, blue-grey eyes, gives me a shy grin. His girlfriend breaks into a radiant smile, clapping her hands with glee.

"What's wrong, Pappa?"

"Nothing, honey."

"Then why are there tears in your eyes?"

epilogue

Jim was kind, loving, and considerate from the moment I met him. He was unfailingly polite and courteous. He was genuinely interested in what you had to say, and he didn't make unkind or sarcastic remarks. He was funny and mischievous, generous and disarmingly shy. He did not seek fame or notoriety. He was a sensitive, tender young man who wrote poetry. He was also a genius who thought deeply, questioned, and sought to understand. This is not a sanitized version of him. It was why Mary loved him. It was the Jim I met and knew and loved.

I have heard embarrassing accounts of how he behaved badly and could be terribly inconsiderate of his band mates and others.

How he could be thoughtless and unreliable. I never witnessed this, but I feel certain that Jim's bad behaviour was fuelled by booze. Jim consumed alcohol until, finally, alcohol consumed Jim.

Mary had wondered if Jim might still be alive had he not had that fateful access to heroin. His drugs of choice, LSD and weed, were not lethal. Jim's problem drug was alcohol. I started imagining how things might have been had he magically ended up in an AA program. He was so intelligent and curious that he might well have responded to their philosophy, which has brought seemingly hopeless cases back from the brink.

What if he had beaten his addiction, confronted his demons, and gone on to a successful career as a poet and writer? Perhaps returning to LA and teaching at his alma mater, UCLA. I wondered if Mary's life would have taken a much different turn. What if they had gotten back together?

Perhaps Mary's art lessons revealed her talent, and she opened a successful studio in Venice, where Jim appears one afternoon after returning from Paris. What if they had gotten back together and followed through on their marriage plans and had a family. Why not? Life is full of improbabilities.

How improbable that my happily married daughters, raised in a small city in British Columbia, both ended up living in LA. And that my grandchildren go to school in Venice.

This Christmas our family went to *The Nutcracker* ballet at the legendary Royce Hall, a majestic twin-towered concert hall on the UCLA campus, ironically the same Royce Hall where the band gave one of their first live performances as the Doors.

As the ballet dancers held the audience spellbound, I gazed along the row in the darkened theatre, watching my innocent grandchildren, their enormous blue eyes captivated by the spectacle. Beside them, my elegant wife and daughters, their lovely faces marvelling at the magic on stage.

I glanced farther along to see another family equally enchanted. I fantasized that it was Mary and Jim with their family. I imagined I was inside Jim's head, remembering when he attended lectures in this magnificent theatre as a student, remembering when he performed here with the Doors. The irony that he is back again, sitting transfixed with his family watching *The Nutcracker* on that very same stage. Marvelling at Tchaikovsky's musical genius, and intrigued that the entire two-act play is performed without a single word being spoken. Leaning over, touching Mary's hand, and smiling at the rapt faces of his grandchildren. Reflecting on his extraordinary life as he nods approvingly at the permanent inscription etched in stone above the stage, celebrating education and knowledge.

THE END

author's note

It was reported that Jim, Jimi Hendrix, and Janis Joplin were all in the same New York nightclub, The Scene, on the same night in March 1968. All three of them died at the same age: twenty-seven. Kurt Cobain's death at twenty-seven gave rise to the so-called "27 Club." Brian Jones of the Rolling Stones died at twenty-seven. Amy Winehouse is the latest member of this unspeakably tragic group.

Jim's will was legally disputed. The estate assets were ultimately split between his mother and father and Pam's mother and father. His estate was recently estimated to be over eighty million dollars. Pam tragically died of a heroin overdose. She was twenty-seven.

acknowledgements

Thank you to my amazing agent, Hilary McMahon, at Westwood Creative Artists. This remarkable woman literally changed my life. Her wisdom, talent, and expertise has been indispensable. Thank you, Hilary, for your encouragement, determination, and guidance, presented with your signature candour and sparkling wit.

Thank you, Westwood Creative, for your professionalism and dedication to your authors. I am privileged to be with an agency so highly regarded by their writers and international network of co-agents and publishers.

What a pleasure to work with the talented team at Dundurn Press. Thank you, Elena Radic, for your exceptional editing, input, and suggestions — and your patience! Thank you to Laura Boyle and her artwork team, who created the clever and evocative cover. Scott Fraser, Kathryn Lane, Rachel Spence: I am grateful for your enthusiastic support from the beginning. Thank you to the sales, marketing, and publicity teams for their diverse skills and talents.

Thank you, Julie, for your feedback and unwavering support.

Heartfelt thanks to the following people: my pivotally supportive friend David Swail, without whom this book would not have seen the light of day; Howard Obrand and Peter Kent — thank you so much for your unrestrained support from day one; John Hagg, always there for me; Chris Paliare, my forever positive and enthusiastic friend; my beloved mentor, John Burrows; Norm Anderson, cherished beyond words; Curly Butler, my side-splitting pal; Aman Soin; and Austin.

I thank my mother for her unconditional love. And thank you to my family for their completely earnest yet totally subjective appraisal of my book as belonging to the "bestseller" category when it was still only half written.

There are two extraordinary girls in my life who have filled me with joy and unbounded love from the day that I met them. They are an entire book of superlatives. I am so grateful for my wonderful, loving, brilliant daughters, Hilary and Whitney.

And last but, of course, not least: to Jim and Mary. Thank you for welcoming me, for your friendship, and your love.

CPSIA information can be obtained
at www.ICGtesting.com
Printed in the USA
JSHW012242161020
8842JS00005B/43

9 781459 746602